# International Financial Reporting Standards and The Tax Implications in Nigeria

Second Edition
**David Kriz Ewoma**

**Kriz David Betterlife Foundation** is a not-for-profit organization committed to meeting the physiological needs of less privileged persons especially the provision of food, providing trainings to individuals to acquire marketable skills and shaping moral values in the society. The foundation currently receives sixty percent of the net proceeds due to The Nitty-Gritty Practice from the launch and sales of this publication.

# Preface

The first edition of IFRS and Tax was a novel idea in Africa to be modest in the field of accountancy and taxation. The concept of the book was to reveal the tax issues accountants, tax practitioners and business owners will be saddled with the adoption of IFRS in Nigeria. Further, the book provided a compass for the Federal and State Tax Authority on what should be done – amendments and alignment of the current tax legislations with IFRS.

This second edition provides up-to-date information and incorporates the various amendments to IFRS, new standards that will be in effect from January 1st, 2013. The tax implications based on amendment to Personal Income Tax, Companies Income Tax and Value Added Tax Acts have been reflected in the relevant chapters. Online access code has also been provided to enable users track updates on IFRS and tax legislations.

We believe that this book will be a veritable tool to tax administrators, practitioners, tax payers and students. We are particularly delighted based on earlier comments that the book offers users the requisite knowledge required to prepare financial statements under IFRS and demonstrable skills for accounting for taxes and filing of tax returns.

Comments regarding errors, omission and improvement for future editions should be sent to kriz@midaspage.com for our consideration.

**Kriz E. David**
Midaspage Consulting
Lagos
December 2012

# Acknowledgement

I am grateful to Dr. Adebola Olubanjo for his invaluable advice and support always.

I want to say a big thank you to my mentors Uche Ogah OON, Dr. Odeyemi Demola, Albert Folorunsho, Ajibade Fashina, Seyi Kumapayi, David C. Alaribe for the indelible marks they have left in my life.

My unreserved appreciation goes to S.S. Ogungbesan, A. J. Bamidele, G. Ogunjemilusi and other directors of the FIRS and the Tax Policy IFRS Working Committee for their feedback on the IFRS project.

I also want to give due recognition and say thank you to my professional colleagues especially my co-lecturers: Samuel Alonge, Taiwo Oyedele and other directors and lecturers at Wyse Associates Limited, Lagos.

# Contents

# Why the move to International Financial Reporting Standards (IFRS)

## 1.1 Introduction

In 2010, the Federal Government of Nigeria accepted the adoption of International Financial Reporting Standards (IFRS) in Nigeria. The adoption of IFRS also facilitated the name change of the local accounting standards setter, the Nigeria Accounting Standards Board (NASB) to the Financial Reporting Council (FRC) that will ensure that corporate entities align with the globally accepted, high-quality accounting standards by fully converting the current National Accounting Standards to International Financial Reporting Standards.

The phase transition to the adoption of IFRS proposed by the FRC will see in Phase 1, Publicly Listed Entities and Significant Public Interest Entities (mostly companies quoted in the Nigerian Stock Exchange) prepare financial statements to comply with IFRS by 31st December 2012. Phase 2, is mandatory adoption by other public interest entities from January 2013 and IFRS for Small and Medium-sized Entities (SMEs) by 31st December 2014 to complete the phase transition.

The adoption of IFRS is more than changing the accounting rules or simply applying new accounting standards. It involves commercial awareness of various industries to enable correct and right interpretations and judgments as the circumstance arises. IFRS adoption will be one of the most fundamental changes that corporate entities will have to deal with over the transition period outlined by the FRC. It is a momentous change that will come with both risk and opportunities. As such, businesses and their regulators need to be prepared and brace up to the new responsibilities that will be posed by the change.

## 1.2 Origin of IFRS

Though the first issue of standards called IFRS was in April 2001 by the International Accounting Standard Board (IASB), a single set of global accounting standards has been under development since the establishment of the International Accounting Standards Committee (IASC) in 1973. The IFRS comprises the modified International Accounting Standards (IAS) and the new standards. IFRS also includes the interpretations issued by the Standing Interpretations Committee (SIC) and the International Financial Reporting Interpretations Committee (IFRIC) and the IASB framework.

## 1.3 The IASB's Objectives

The importance and the objectives of IASB for introducing IFRS are:

- To develop, in the public interest, a single set of high quality, understandable and enforceable global accounting standards that require high quality, transparent and comparable information in financial statements and other financial reporting to help participants in the various capital markets of the world and other users of the information to make economic decisions.

- To promote the use and rigorous application of those standards;

- To work actively with national standard-setters to bring about convergence of national accounting standards and IFRS to high quality solutions.

The recent unprecedented global financial crisis has further fostered the need for convergence of national and international accounting standards. It is believed with the adoption of IFRS the financial statements of two similar companies in the different countries would be comparable thus 'speaking the same language' in that:

- The financial statements would represent faithfully events and transactions that management of companies must (not choose) report as at when they happened.

- The financial statements should account for like transactions and events in the like manner and account for different transactions and events differently.

The IFRS are principles-based standards that deal with most of the events, transactions and structures obtainable in practice and allow management and auditors of companies to use their professional judgment in applying the principles to those areas not specifically covered but should be in compliance with the IASB framework.

## 1.4 The IASB's Framework

The framework is the bedrock for the development of accounting standards. It requires financial statements prepared under IFRS to meet the following objectives: to communicate financial position, performance and cash flow and to report on the five elements of accounting which are assets, liabilities, equity, income and expenses. Financial Statements should provide information about an entity which will be relevant to a wide range of users in making economic decisions and to report the results of management's stewardship of the resources entrusted to it. To achieve the objectives the framework leans heavily towards reporting.

*Position over performance*: This dominates the IFRS framework via the definition and the recognition criteria of assets and liabilities.

An asset is defined as 'a resource controlled by the entity as a result of past events and from which future economic benefits are expected to flow to the entity'

A liability is 'a present obligation of the entity arising from past events, the settlement of which is expected to result in an outflow from the entity of resources embodying economic benefits'

The IASB argues that the financial performance of an entity is the movement between two financial positions.

*Fair Value over Historical Cost*: Historical cost values assets at their historical cost using the nominal currency as its measurement unit. Fair value was defined as 'the amount for which an asset could be exchanged, or a liability settled, between knowledgeable, willing parties in an arm's length transaction.' IFRS13 defined fair value as 'the price received to sell an asset or paid to transfer a liability in an orderly transaction, between market participants at the measurement date.' Further discussion on fair value measurement is in Chapter three.

The IASB prefers the use of fair value accounting and argues that while historical cost accounting provides a reliable basis for measurement, fair value accounting offers relevant information; and for information to be useful for economic or investment decision it has to be relevant.

## 1.5 Rationale for IFRS Adoption

The rationale for adopting IFRS hinges on the perceived benefits that would accrue to an economy when corporate entities report using a single high quality global set of accounting standards. These benefits include accessibility to global capital markets due to the increased comparability of financial statements arising from applying IFRS, improved global competitiveness and reduction of cost of capital. The availability of reliable useful and relevant information on various investment portfolios which consequently attracts Foreign Direct Investment becomes inevitable.

Conversion to IFRS will facilitate easy consolidation of financial information of the same company with offices in different countries and easier regulation of financial information of entities. Further, the cost of doing business across borders will be reduced and thus improve profitability.

## 1.6 Impact of IFRS adoption on Business Operations

The changes driven by the adoption of IFRS will impact on the entire business operations and processes. A successful conversion project will therefore require an enterprise approach or a top-down approach with the full commitment of the directors of the companies.

### Corporate Planning

The strategic intent of an entity sets the sail for the type of information that its processes will strive to produce. The conversion to IFRS will give rise to revision of an entity's long and mid-term strategic plans, in order to provide the necessary data or information to meet IFRS reporting disclosures.

IFRS adoption will also affect the frequency with which corporate plans and objectives are drafted because of the volatility of information from capital markets and the business operations that require management judgments. Internal budgeting and forecasting will need to be reappraised often based on the new assets and liabilities recognition and measurement rules.

### Information Technology System

The conversion to IFRS will require huge investments on information technology as a result of the new reporting requirements. IFRS robust disclosures and presentations needs will necessitate new investment in IT in order to capture new data required for management judgment and decision.

During the transition period, there would be need to maintain dual records both of the local GAAP and IFRS. The existing IT system may not have the capacity to maintain the records and there is the need to ensure information reliability and system security.

### Business Policies and Processes

Entities would be forced to review their business policies and adopt new policies that comply with IFRS requirements. This will inevitably affect current business procedures or the processing of transactions.

Most manual processes will have to be automated to be able to produce timely information for valuations and measurement for reporting purposes.

### Internal Control Procedures
A wide range of controls will be introduced and re-documentation of internal control procedures especially relating to financial reporting on financial instruments, property plant and equipment, investment properties and valuation. Documentation of new accounting policies and procedure manuals will be necessary.

### Corporate Governance
IFRS adoption will give rise to new reporting structures and reporting functions. This will impact on the existing governance committees such as the audit committee, remuneration committee etc functions. Management boards may be reorganized to facilitate information generation for the exercise of correct judgments and to ensure adequate controls and certification of procedures due to the robust disclosure under IFRS.

### Treasury Function
The treasury function will be impacted given the variety of criteria for evaluating hedging or hedged items, especially securitization and recognition/de-recognition of financial instruments.

### Investor Relations
A lot more communications on capital market will be inevitable. The justification for the choice of accounting policies for example cost model over fair value or otherwise to financial analysts and investors. Also, timely and detailed analysis to explain the volatility or the changes in financial statements as a result of reporting under IFRS will be expected.

## 1.7 Impact of IFRS adoption on Corporate and Financial Reporting

Technically, conversion to IFRS is more than just a financial reporting issue or mere changes of accounting rules and standards. The following are some ways IFRS adoption will impact on corporate and financial reporting:

### Performance reporting
The changes brought about by the IFRS on recognition and measurement of transactions will impact on the parameters used by companies and investors in assessing corporate performance.

### Increased transparency and comparability
One of the objectives the IASB seeks to achieve when entities prepare their financial statements under IFRS is high quality transparency and comparability. This is achieved with increased volume of disclosure requirement under IFRS.

### Increased complexity in financial reporting
The preparation of financial statements under IFRS will be a lot more tedious compared to the requirements under the local GAAP. For example the increased use of discounting techniques in valuations would be complex processes to accountants.

### Volatility of financial reporting
There would be potential increased volatility in reporting financial results with the adoption of IFRS. IFRS offers some optional basis for recognition and measurement, for example a company may choose the revaluation or cost model in reporting tangible non-current assets.

### Volatility of financial ratios and key performance indicators
This will arise due to selection between historical cost accounting and fair value accounting. Most key performance indicators used by credit providers are closely tied to existing financial covenants, for example adjustments passed on equity would impact on the debt to equity ratios which may affect credit facilities agreements.

**Executive and employee performance measurement**
Performance based pay linked to earnings, profitability or share prices will be affected with the adoptions of IFRS. It is expected that the financial performance or earnings, earnings per share and the financial position will change. This would give rise to renegotiation of new compensation plan by employees.

**Transitional impact on bottom line**
Conversion to IFRS will have significant impact on bottom line and financial position of companies during the transition years. The write offs and write back as well as the recognition and de-recognition of assets and liabilities at first time adoption of IFRS will justify the change.

## 1.8 Impact of IFRS adoption on Tax reporting and Filing

The adoption of IFRS will give rise to several issues that will impact on tax accounting and cash tax payment to the Inland Revenue. Converting to IFRS will impact on both current and deferred tax. Outlined below are some of the potential impacts:

**Current Taxes**
Tax laws are the basis for assessing companies to tax in Nigeria and are creations of Acts of Parliament while financial statements are prepared in accordance with generally accepted accounting principles (GAAP) which in this case is the IFRS.

Currently there is no alignment between the Nigerian Local GAAP and the Tax Laws, though the starting point for tax computation is the accounting profit reported in the financial statements. The adoption of IFRS will pose serious adjustments in tax computation for filing purposes which will adversely impact on tax payers' profit. Examples of some of the challenges include: revenue recognition, fair value adjustments, impairment, testing, provision on risk assets and the likes. Details of the tax implications on each accounting standard are dealt with in the respective chapters.

## Deferred Tax

IFRS adoption will impact on deferred tax accounting of companies. In particular, the values of timing differences and the time frame over which they are expected to reverse. The volatility in value of assets giving rise to new carrying values for assets at reporting periods will significantly impact on the evaluation of deferred tax.

The transition to IFRS, the re-preparation of financial statements to reset the accounts balances to comply with IFRS will give rise to significant deferred tax accounting issues. For example the de-recognition/recognition of assets and liabilities in accounts, writing offs/write back of provisions or balances to the relevant components of financial statements. Detailed deferred tax implications are covered in the relevant chapters.

### References

IFRS RED Book 2012 PART A: 'The Conceptual Framework and Requirements' and PART B: 'The Accompanying Documents' Conceptual Framework for Financial Reporting
Barry Elliott and Jamie Elliott (2006) Financial Accounting, Reporting and Analysis, International Edition 2nd Edition Prentice Hall Financial Times
Report of the committee on Road Map to the Adoption of International Financial Reporting Standards in Nigeria
Midaspage, Nigeria (2010) Tax Consequences of Adopting IFRS in Nigeria

# 2

## IFRS 1: First time adoption of IFRS

### 2.1 Introduction

This is the standard that deals with the implementation of IFRS for the time. It applies to an entity that adopts IFRS for the first time and makes an explicit and unreserved statement that its general purpose financial statements comply with IFRS.

Financial statements that comply with some (but not all) IFRS or financial statements in local GAAP with reconciliation to IFRS, do not meet the criteria of first-time IFRS financial statements.

The standard sets out the procedures that an entity must follow when it adopts IFRS for the first time. The general principle is that the first time financial statement should be prepared on the basis that the entity had always applied IFRS. This is in effect retrospective application. However, as it may be difficult, expensive or impossible to rigidly apply this principle, the standard contains some important exceptions and exemptions to the basic measurement principles of some other IFRS.

### 2.2 Transition Period

There is sometimes confusion between what the standard refers to as the 'first reporting date' and the 'transition date'. For example; A company with 31st December as year-end wishes to adopt IFRS for the first time in 2012; the first financial statements prepared under IFRS will be for the year ended 31st December 2012 called the first reporting date.

However, the financial statements will present comparative figures for the full year ended 31st December 2011. So the first date IFRS will be adopted is the beginning of the comparative period, which is 1st January 2011 called the transition date.

The practical issue here is that for the reporting period ending 31st December 2011, two separate accounting books have to be maintained in the previous GAAP and the IFRS.

**IFRS First Adoption Timeline**

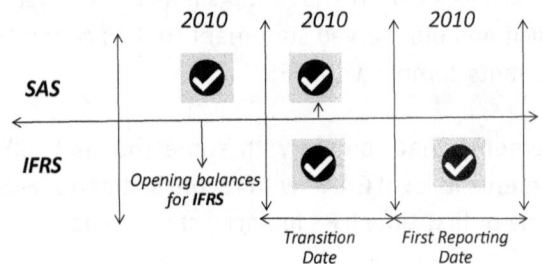

Figure 2.1: First Time Adoption Timeline

From the above we can deduce the following practical steps or procedures for financial reporting during the transition period.

Statement of Financial Position under SAS as at 31st December 2010
Financial Statements using SAS as at 31st December 2011
Statement of Financial Position under IFRS as at 1st January 2011
Statement of Financial Position under IFRS as at 31st December 2011

### 2.3 IFRS Conversion Timeline

Giving the phase transition road map proposed by the Financial Reporting Council (FRC), below are examples of the transition period for IFRS conversion for some companies in the first phase in Nigeria:

| Year End | First Reporting Date | Transition Date |
|---|---|---|
| 31 December | 31 December, 2012 | 1 January, 2011 |
| 31 March | 31 March, 2013 | 1 April, 2011 |
| 30 June | 30 June, 2013 | 1 July, 2011 |
| 30 September | 30 September, 2013 | 1 October, 2011 |

Figure 2.2: IFRS Transition Dates

## 2.4 Transition Process

**Accounting policies:** The entity will have to select the accounting policies that comply with IFRS in force at the reporting date.

*De-recognition of existing assets and liabilities:* The financial statement prepared under the previous GAAP will have some assets and liabilities that do not qualify for recognition under IFRS. For example, IFRS do not permit the recognition of following as assets: research, start-up and pre-operating cost, staff training, deferred advertising expenditure and relocation cost. Liabilities not permitted to be recognized under IFRS are general or contingency provisions, future restructuring cost and operating losses and provisions for major overhauls of assets.

*Recognition of new assets and liabilities:* IFRS may require the recognition of assets and liabilities that were not recognized under previous GAAP. The most important of these are likely to be derivative financial assets and liabilities, and deficits or surpluses under defined benefit plans. These would include not just pension plans but also items such as medical care cost and life insurance. Other recognizable liabilities might be deferred tax balances and certain provisions such as environmental and decommissioning costs.

*Reclassification of assets and liabilities:* Assets and liabilities recognized under previous GAAP may need to be reclassified under IFRS. For example:
a.    Certain intangible assets, recognized on a business combination, would need to be reclassified as goodwill if

their recognition does not meet IAS 38 Intangible Assets criteria. It is also possible that the reverse could occur.

b.   Items classified as share capital may need to be reclassified as debt. IAS 32 requires redeemable preference share to be classified as debt and compound financial instrument (e.g. convertible loan notes) may have to be split between debt and equity.

c.   Some investments that may not have been consolidated under previous GAAP may meet the definition of a subsidiary under IFRS and have to be consolidated.

**Measurement:** The value at which some assets and liabilities are measured will change under the IFRS e.g. Fair value and cost model. The net effect of the above adjustments should be recognized in retained earnings or other appropriate category of equity.

**Exemptions:** IFRS 1 grants exemptions on the above principles where the cost of compliance would outweigh the benefits to users. These are made up of optional and mandatory exemptions. See appendix 1 for detailed list of exemptions.

**Disclosures:** IFRS 1 requires disclosures that explain how the transition to IFRS has affected the entity's financial position, income statement and cash flow. This is achieved through:

a.   A reconciliation of equity under previous GAAP to equity under IFRS both at the date of transition and at the end of the last reporting period under previous GAAP. If adoption of IFRS was in the year ended 31st December 2012 then this would be at 1st January 2011 and 31st December 2011.

b.   A reconciliation of profit from previous GAAP to IFRS for the last reported period under previous GAAP. For the above, this would be 31st December 2011.

c.   The reconciliations should be supplemented by explanations and disclosure of:

- Material adjustments made to financial statements in adopting IFRS for the first time.
- Correction of errors discovered in previous GAAP
- The recognition or reversal of any impairment losses inpreparing the opening statement of financial positions;
- Any specific exemptions it has elected to use under IFRS 1

## 2.5 Tax Implications

IFRS 1 specifies the process of re-setting account balances which is the preparation of the opening Statement of Financial Position. The tax implications that will arise are outlined below:

### Deferred tax
The recognition and de-recognition of assets and liabilities will involve writing off and write back balances which will result to new carrying values for such assets and liabilities. This will impact on the deferred tax balance of the companies.

### Corporation tax
The possibility of re-computing the income tax is remote. IFRS 1 specified that all adjustments arising from resetting of account balances should be debited or credited to equity.

The adjustments through equity may however distort one of the parameters for computing minimum tax for companies under the Companies Income Tax Act Cap C21 2004 LFN.

The Tax Authority will request for the statement of reconciliation from Statement of Accounting Standard (SAS) to IFRS and journal entries passed to recognize or remove or reclassify assets and liabilities.

## References

IFRS RED Book 2012 PART A: 'The Conceptual Framework and Requirements' and PART B: 'The Accompanying Documents'
    IFRS1 First Time Adoption of International Financial Reporting Standards
Companies Income Tax Act Cap C21 2004 LFN
Midaspage, Nigeria (2010) Tax Consequences of Adopting IFRS in Nigeria

# IFRS 13: Fair Value Measurement

## 3.1 Introduction

The IASB sets out in a single IFRS framework; IFRS 13 Fair Value Measurement, when another IFRS permits or requires the application or the use of fair value for measuring financial elements in the preparation of financial statements.

IFRS 13 defines fair value as 'the price that would be received to sell an asset or paid to transfer a liability in an orderly transaction between market participants at the measurement date'. The measurement and disclosure requirements of IFRS 13 do not cover fair value based transactions like:

- Share-based payments within the scope of IFRS 2 Share-Based Payment.
- Leases within the scope of IAS 17 Leases.
- The application of net realizable value within the scope of IAS 2 Inventories.
- The application of value-in-use within the scope of IAS 36 Impairment of Assets.

## 3.2 The Application of Fair Value Measurement

The definition of fair value underscores that fair value is a market-based measurement rather than an entity specific measurement. The IASB stresses that fair value under IFRS 13 is the exit price for assets and liabilities taking into consideration the assumptions that market participants would use when pricing an asset or a liability at the prevailing market conditions including risks associated with the asset or liability.

This implies that, an entity's intention to hold an asset or to settle or otherwise fulfill a liability is irrelevant when carrying out fair value measurement. Fair value measurement requires an entity to determine the following:

- The characteristics of the asset or liability to be measured,
- The market in which an orderly transaction would take place for the asset or liability,
- The assumptions that market participants that is buyers and sellers would used in pricing the asset or liability in a principal or most advantageous market,
- For a non-financial asset, the highest and best use of the asset and whether the asset is used in combination with other assets or on a stand-alone basis,
- The appropriate valuation technique(s) that will maximize the use of relevant observable inputs and minimize unobservable inputs.

### 3.3 Transfer of a Liability or Entity's Own Equity

Fair value measurement assumes that a financial or non-financial liability or an entity's own equity instrument is transferred to a market participant at the measurement date. The hypothetical transfer assumes that:

- A liability would remain outstanding and the market participant transferee would be required to fulfill the obligation. The liability would not be settled with the counterparty or otherwise extinguished on the measurement date.
- An entity's own equity instrument would remain outstanding and the market participant transferee would take on the rights and responsibilities associated with the instrument. The instrument would not be cancelled or otherwise extinguished on the measurement date.

### 3.4. Fair Value Measurement Valuation Techniques

IFRS 13 prescribes three valuation techniques an entity can adopt for fair value measurement. An entity is expected to use the appropriate valuation technique(s) for which sufficient data are available to measure fair value, maximizing the use of relevant observable inputs and minimizing the use of unobservable inputs. The valuation techniques are:

- **Market Approach:** This approach uses prices and other relevant information generated by market transaction involving identical or comparable/similar asset, liabilities, or a group of assets and liabilities.
- **Cost Approach:** This approach reflects the amount that would be required currently to replace the service capacity of an asset usually referred to as replacement cost.
- **Income Approach:** This approach converts future amounts; cash inflows and outflows to a single current/discounted amount, reflecting current market expectations about those future amounts.

**Scenario 3.1 Fair Value Measurement**

On January 1st 2009, a non financial asset with an estimated useful life of 10 years was acquired for N18million. As at $31^{st}$ December 2010, the price that will be received to asset was N15million, and the cost of a new model of that asset was N21million. With cost of capital of 10% the existing asset is expected to generate N2.4million annually for the remaining useful life of the asset. Evaluate Financial Statement and Tax Effects.

The carrying value of the non financial asset using historical cost as at December 31, 2010 is N14.4million (N18m – N3.6). Using the market approach, the quote price of the asset at the measurement date was N15million. In the event that there is no active market for the asset, the fair value of the asset for financial reporting purpose will be N16.8million (N21m – N4.2m) or N12.8million (N2.4m * 5.335) using the cost and income approach valuation techniques respectively.

The capital allowance rates for a non financial asset with a useful life of 10 years is 15% and 10% for initial and annual allowance respectively. The tax base of the asset as December 31, 2010 will be N12.2million. Capital allowance will be grant of the cost of the asset. The fair value of the asset will give rise to a taxable temporary difference as at the reporting date.

## 3.5 Hierarchy of Fair Value Inputs

The inputs used in the valuation techniques are categorized into a fair value hierarchy with a view to seeking consistency and comparability of the results of fair value measurements. The hierarchy gives the highest priority to unadjusted quoted prices in active markets for identical assets or liabilities and the lowest level to unobservable inputs. The levels of inputs are as follows:

- **Level 1 Inputs**: Are quoted prices in active market for identical assets or liabilities that the entity can access at the measurement date. The actual price quoted in an active market for assets and liabilities will provide the most reliable evidence of the value of such assets and liabilities.

- **Level 2 Inputs**: Are inputs other than quoted market prices that are observable for the asset or liability, either directly or indirectly, examples include quoted prices for similar/identical assets or liabilities in active or not active market or other observable indices such as interest rates and yield curves.

- **Level 3 inputs**: Are unobservable inputs used to the extent that relevant observable inputs are not available. The entity can use its own assumptions about the market exit value.

## 3.6 Tax Implications

**Transition period**

The will be a growth or depletion of retained earnings for any entity that chose fair value or revaluation model as deemed cost for all or some class of item of property, plant and equipment, intangible assets and investment property as a result of transition adjustments.

Transition adjustments giving rise to a growth in retained earnings will create additional tax on dividend payout. Minimum tax payment will also be effected whether there is a growth or depletion of retained earnings.

## Current tax

Fair value gains or losses credited or charged to the profit or loss statement will be adjusted for in the determination of assessable profit. If the tax authority decides to tax fair value gains, fair value would be allowed as a deductible expense. In other case, the effects of fair value measurement should be disregarded for income tax computation.

## Deferred tax

The carrying values of assets and liabilities will be affected as a result of fair value measurement at each reporting date while the tax base of such assets will remain unchanged except for annual allowances provided for in the tax laws. The detail treatment of deferred tax is covered in chapter 20.

## References

IFRS RED Book 2012 PART A: 'the conceptual framework and requirements' and PART B: 'the accompanying documents'
    IFRS 13 Fair Value Measurement
Companies Income Tax Act Cap C21 2004 LFN
Midaspage Tax and IFRS Academy (2012) IFRS: Tax Implications

# IAS 1: Presentation of Financial Statements

## 4.1 Introduction

IAS 1 provides guidance on the overall structure of the financial statements including the minimum requirements for each primary statement. These requirements are supplemented by the specific requirements of other standards. A complete set of IFRS financial statements (see appendices for detail) should comprise the following with equal prominence:

- Statement of Financial Position as at the end of the period
- Statement of Profit or Loss and Other Comprehensive Income
- Statement of Changes in Equity for the period
- Statement of Cash Flows for the period
- Notes, comprising a summary of significant accounting policies and other explanatory information

## 4.2 Statement of Financial Position

This was formerly known as the balance sheet. It communicates the financial position of an entity at each reporting date. It shows Assets, Liabilities and Equity.

Current/Non-current distinction: IAS 1 requires an asset or liability to be classified as current where:
- It will be settled within 12 months of the reporting date; or
- It is held for the purpose of trading; or
- It is part of the entity's normal operating cycle

The implication is that for companies that provide extended credit facilities or sales, the receivables would be classified as current, even where credit term extends more than one year

**Equity:** This comprises share capital and reserves. IAS 1 aggregates reserves other than retained earnings into other components of equity such as share premium reserve, revaluation reserve, general reserve etc.

## 4.3  Statement of Profit or Loss and Other Comprehensive Income

IAS 1 requires companies to provide a performance statement which reports profit or loss and other comprehensive income in a single statement or two separate statements as profit or loss statement and other comprehensive income.

**Profit or Loss Statement**: provides details information about income and expenses during the reporting period. Below is a summary of the profit or loss statement:
- Operating
- Exceptional
- Financing
- Tax

**Exceptional items:**  are certain material income or expense items required to be disclosed on the face of the income statement before operating profit from operations. Extraordinary item does not exist under IFRS as such; all items including exceptional items are deemed to arise from ordinary activities.

Examples of exceptional items are:
- Write down/reversal of inventories to net realizable value
- Impairments/reversal of property, plant and equipment
- Restructuring provisions or their reversal
- Disposals of items of property, plant and equipment
- Disposals of investments

- Settlement of litigation
- Discontinued operations (group financial statement)

**Other Comprehensive Income:** comprises items of income and expenses that are not recognized in profit or loss as required or permitted by other IFRS. The items to be reported in other comprehensive income include:
- Revaluation gains and losses on property, plant and equipment.
- Gains and losses on re-measuring available-for-sale financial assets.
- Actuarial gains and losses on defined benefit plans recognized.
- Gains and losses arising from translation of financial statements of foreign operation.
- The portion of gains and losses on hedging instruments that are effective cash flow hedges.

### 4.4 Statement of Changes in Equity

This links the statements of financial position and comprehensive income. It shows the changes in equity in the period arising from transactions between the entity and its owners. It highlights, new shares issued and dividend payment. All other changes in equity during the period are due to activities from the income statements and other comprehensive income.

### 4.5 Tax Implications

The classification of items in the components of financial statement as required in IAS 1 (revised) would give arise to the following tax issues

### Determination of tax liability

Under the local GAAP, determination of income tax liability is easier. The current format of statement of profit or loss and other comprehensive income will make income tax computation a complex task; the adjustment from the accounting profit to tax profit would involving fishing out relevant information or figures distributed all over the statement of profit or loss and other comprehensive income. The treatment of both realized and unrealized profit reported from fair value valuations on financial instrument through the profit and loss account and investment properties are examples.

Exceptional items constitute items that are liable to both income tax and capital gains tax. It will require higher skill to ascertain this distinction. Further, disposal of property plant and equipment item would require the application of the Value Added Tax provision.

The current position of the income tax law does not permit charge against income as a write off from non-current assets. While depreciation charge is replaced with capital allowance claim, there is no allowance for impairment of assets. Besides, impairment of assets could be on individual assets as well as cash generating units (CGU).

IAS 1 requires that the tax effects on items reported in other comprehensive income should be captured in that section. The total tax effect can be reported as a line item or the net of tax of the items can be reported. However, just like exceptional items; the items are liable to Income Tax, Capital Gains Tax and Value Added Tax.

**Tax on dividend**
The statement of changes in equity captures the amount of dividend paid in a given reporting period. While it was easy to ascertain the amount of dividend that is attributable to current year profit for the purpose of comparison with the total profit for tax purpose, the figure of dividend that would be reported in the statement of changes in equity may be accumulation of profits from several years. This may give rise to tracing to ascertain the portion of dividend attributable to current year's profit.

**Minimum tax provision**
The parameters for computing minimum tax may be distorted with the new arrangement of the components of the Statement of Profit or Loss and Other Comprehensive Income.

## References

IFRS RED Book 2012 PART A: 'the conceptual framework and requirements' and PART B: 'the accompanying documents'

IAS 1 Presentation of Financial Statements

Companies Income Tax Act Cap C21 2004 LFN

Midaspage, Nigeria (2010) Tax Consequences of Adopting IFRS in Nigeria

# IAS 18: Revenue Recognition

## 5.1 Introduction

The IASB framework for the preparation and presentation of financial statements defines income as:

*'...increases in economic benefits during the accounting period <u>in the form of inflows or enhancements of assets or decreases of liabilities</u> that result in increase in equity, other than those relating to contributions from equity participants.'*

Revenue is a subset of income and is defined in IAS 18 as:
*'..the gross inflow of economic benefits during the period arising in <u>the course of the ordinary activities</u> of an entity when those inflows result in increases in equity, other than increases relating to contributions from equity participants.'*

The framework explains that income encompasses both revenue and gains. Revenue is referred to by various names including sales, fees, interest, dividends, royalties and rent. Gains are other items that meet the definition of income, such as those arising on the disposal of non-current assets, for example, property, plant and equipment or long-term investments. They also include revaluation surpluses arising from revaluation of marketable securities or fixed assets.

Changes in equity that relate to contributions from or distributions to owners are excluded from the definitions of income and expense. Capital contributions should be presented in the statement of changes in equity. Such contributions are not gains and therefore should not be reported in the Profit or Loss Statement.

## 5.2 Timing of Recognition

IAS 18 distinguishes between revenue from the sale of goods, revenue from the rendering of services and revenue from the use by others of the entity's assets.

**Sale of goods**: Revenue should be recognized when all the following conditions have been satisfied:
- The entity has transferred to the buyer the significant risks and rewards of ownership of the goods.
- The entity does not retain either continuing managerial involvement to the degree usually associated with ownership or effective control over the goods sold.
- The amount of revenue can be measured reliably.
- It is probable that the economic benefits associated with the transaction will flow to the entity.
- The cost incurred or to be incurred in respect of the sale can be measured reliably.

If the entity retains significant risk of ownership, the transaction is not a sale and revenue is not recognized. An entity may retain a significant risk of ownership in a number of ways:

- When the entity retains an obligation for unsatisfactory performance not covered by normal warranty provisions
- When the receipt of the revenue from a particular sale is contingent on the derivation of revenue by the buyer from its sale of the goods
- When the goods are shipped subject to installation and the installation is a significant part of the contract which has not yet been completed by the entity; and
- When the buyer has right to rescind the purchase for a reason specified in the sales contract and the entity is uncertain about the probability of return.

**Sale of services:** When the outcome of the transaction can be estimated reliably, revenue should be recognized by reference to the transaction's stage of completion at the reporting date. The transaction's outcome can be estimated reliably when all the following conditions are satisfied:

- The amount of revenue can be measured reliably.
- It is probable that the economic benefits associated with the transaction will flow to the entity.
- The transaction's stage of completion at the reporting date can be measured reliably.
- The costs incurred and the costs to complete the transaction can be measured reliably.

**Use of assets:** Yielding interest, royalties and dividend should be recognized when:

- It is probable that the economic benefits associated with the transaction will flow to the entity
- The amount of the revenue can be measured reliably
- Interest is recognized using the effective interest method as set out in IAS 39
- Royalties are recognized on an accrual basis in accordance with the substance of the relevant agreement
- Dividends are recognized when the shareholder's right to receive payment is established

### 5.3  Measurement of Revenue

IAS 18 states that revenue is measured at the fair value of the consideration received or receivable. Revenue is usually determined by agreement between the entity and the buyer of the goods. It is measured at the fair value of the consideration received taking into account the amount of any trade discounts or volume rebates allowed.

**Financing transactions:** When the inflow of cash or cash equivalents is deferred, the fair value of the consideration may be less than the nominal amount of cash received or receivable. For example, an entity providing interest free credit to the buyer.

The arrangement effectively constitutes a financing transaction; the fair value of the consideration is determined by discounting all future receipts using an imputed rate of interest

The difference between the fair value of the consideration and the nominal amount of the consideration is recognized as interest revenue.

### Scenario 5.1: Financing Transaction

EMA Ltd deals on plants and fixtures. On 4th February 2009 sold plant for N100 million which cost N75million. EMA Ltd has accepted to receive payment within two years in two equal installments at the end of each year. The nominal interest rate is 16%. Evaluate the financial statements and tax effect.

The transaction is a sale of goods and there is a transfer of significant risks and rewards of ownership of the plant to the buyer at the point of sale. The amount of revenue can be reliably measured and it is probable that economic benefits will flow, so EMA can recognize revenue. However, the installment payment arrangement constitutes a financing transaction. The transaction should be unbundled into revenue (sale of plant) and financing (interest income).

At the end of 2009, EMA Ltd will report in its Financial Statements a Revenue of N80.3million (the present value of expected cash flow discounted using the nominal interest rate) and other income of N12.8million as finance income in the profit or loss statement.

A receivable of N43.1million will be reported in the statement of financial position.

The sale of plant is a taxable supply and would attract VAT at rate of 5%. By unbundling the transaction, VAT of N4.0million (5% of N80.3million) is due as VAT payment to the Revenue. The financing income will not attract VAT. Corporation tax at 32% on the profit (N93.1million less N75.0million) in 2009 accounts as income and education tax on the transaction will be due to the Revenue.

**Exchange of goods:** When goods or services are exchanged or swapped for goods or services of a similar nature and value the exchange is not regarded as a transaction which generates revenue.

When goods are sold or services are rendered in exchange for dissimilar goods or services, the exchange is regarded as a transaction which generates revenue.

Revenue will be measured as the fair value of the goods or services received, adjusted by the amount of any cash or cash equivalents transferred. When the fair value of the goods or services received cannot be measured reliably, the revenue is measured as the fair value of the goods or services given up adjusted by the amount of any cash or cash equivalents transferred.

**Multiple element transactions:** A transaction may contain separately identifiable components that should be accounted for separately. IAS 18 states that, it is necessary to apply the revenue recognition criteria to each separate identifiable component of a single transaction in order to reflect the transaction's substance.

IAS 18 gives an example of a product sold with an obligation for subsequent servicing and states that the amount attributable to the subsequent servicing should be deferred and recognized over the period during which the service is performed.

The principles in IAS 18 require that the revenue in respect of each separable component of a transaction is measured at its fair value. The price that is regularly charged for an item when sold separately is often the best evidence of its fair value.

**Customer Loyalty Programmes:** This is where points earned through the purchase of goods or services can only be redeemed for goods and services provided by the issuing entity. Examples are airlines that offer free air miles and supermarkets that offer loyalty cards that accumulate points that can be used to reduce the cost of future purchases.

The fair value of the consideration received or receivable in respect of the initial sale is allocated between the award credits and the other components of the sale. IFRIC 13 did not specify how to determine fair value but could be estimated using the discount that the customer would obtain when redeeming the incentive for goods and services.

### Scenario 5.2: Multiple elements and customer loyalty transactions

Fly-Jet Ltd operates a loyalty scheme. If a passenger flies two trips a voucher is given that makes the third trip attract a discount of 90% provided the trips are within three months. The cost of a return ticket is N50, 000.00 which is considered as a trip. Evaluate financial statement and tax effects.

The cost of a trip with the airline constitutes a multiple element transaction which is the ticket and the voucher. For a passenger who satisfies the condition, a total consideration of N150, 000.00 for the three trips will be allocated to the components based on their fair values. N45, 000.00 will be allocated to the voucher which is the fair value to the passenger while the balance of N105, 000.00 is allocated as sales for the three trips.

The tax effect will not be daunting if the trips are carried within the same financial year. The flight tickets are taxable supplies, the VAT payable would be N5, 250 (5% of N105, 000) and the income and education tax would be 32% of the profit margin. It is important to point out that where the trips span across two financial years; revenue and tax should be split and recognized for the separate accounting periods.

**Financial services fees**: Financial service fees arise in many forms, including transactions such as loan origination fees, commitment fees and management or performance fees in relation to funds and unit trusts.

The basis for revenue recognition depends on the nature and substance of the services provided as well as the subsequent basis of accounting for any related financial instrument.

- Fees that are integral part of the effective interest rate such as fee for assessing the financial position of the borrower, evaluating and recording guarantees, collateral and other security. These are referred to as origination fees relating to the creation or acquisition of a financial asset (other than FVTPL) together with any direct cost are deferred and recognized as an adjustment to the effective interest rate.

- Fees charged for servicing a loan or investment management fees. These are recognized as revenue as the services are provided.

- Fees earned upon the execution of a significant act. Revenue should be recognized when the act has been performed e.g. fee receivable for sourcing finance or arranging a loan.

### Scenario 5.3: Loan origination fee

MidasBank, grants N10million loan to a merchant on January 1, 2010 repayable at the end of five years. The merchant is charged a fee of N200, 000.00 payable on the date of the transaction as cost giving rise to loan. The current market interest rate is 8%. Evaluate financial statement and tax effects.

The fee charged by MidasBank is an integral part of establishing the N10million. The N200, 000.00 is a loan origination fee to be deferred and recognized as an adjustment to the effective interest rate. Using a discounting cash flow method, the effective interest rate will be 8.51%

to be used in discounting cash flows, the principal of N10million and N800,000.00 in five years to the present value of N9.8million. The effective interest rate of 8.51% will be used to recognize finance cost on the carrying amount of the loan at each year.

The interest income earned by MidasBank is liable to corporation tax at rate of 32%. Financial services giving rise to non-interest income such as fees and commission are taxable supplies. However, loan origination fee is used as integral part of the effective interest rate will not be liable to VAT.

## 5.4 Tax Implications

While IAS 18 provides the distinction between income that are revenue and gains, the tax status provides guidance on when a 'business receipt' could be deemed as revenue or capital receipts. A key distinguishing factor is the recurrence of receipts to businesses. Receipts that recur can be classified as revenue while those that occur once could be capital except as specifically defined in the various tax laws. Income accruing to an entity will have the following tax implications:

- All revenue receipts from the sale of goods, services and the use of assets by third party would be liable to income and education tax in Nigeria.

- Capital receipts are subject to tax under the Capital Gains Tax Act accordingly. It is important to posit that some transactions could have both income tax and capital gains tax implications. For example the proceeds realized from the disposal of a used building would give rise to balancing charge which is taxable under the Income Tax Act and as chargeable gain taxable under the Capital Gains Tax Act.

- In determining the revenue that would be liable to income tax, the Revenue would have to review the contract agreement giving rise to the revenue recognized in the profit or loss statement. Given the stage of completion clause, cash receipts may not necessarily equal to revenue that will be liable to income tax in the year of assessment under review. The practice of using bank statements to validate turnover reported in companies financial statements may not suffice under IFRS reporting framework.

- Interest is a revenue receipt therefore liable to income tax except as may be exempted from tax by other provisions in the Income Tax Act. Most interest income suffer tax deduction at source which is advance payment of income tax but for individual, such tax withheld is regarded as the final tax.

- Dividend income is revenue but treated as franked investment income therefore exempted from tax. Dividend income suffers tax deduction at source. The Revenue would request for the dividend warrant or letter of advice where the income is credited directly into the reporting entity's bank account to certify that the dividend was actually earned.

- Royalty is revenue in nature therefore liable to income tax. Where the receipt is probable, royalty is accrued for on a straight line basis. Royalty is a taxable supply therefore liable to VAT at the current rate. Royalty payments also suffer tax deduction at source at the rate of 10% for payment to companies and 5% for payments to individuals.

- Most transactions on sale of goods and services would be liable to Value Added Tax except as specifically exempted in the VAT Act and FIRS circulars. VAT is to be charged on the net revenue receivable by the entity where transactions are discounted either as trade discount, customer loyalty schemes, multiple element transactions etc. Also, some fees would not be liable to VAT due to the application of effective interest rate in their recognition. The implication is that though such charges are called fees, they are interest in nature.

## References

IFRS RED Book 2012 PART A: 'the conceptual framework and requirements' and PART B: 'the accompanying documents'
    IAS 18: Revenue Recognition
    IFRIC13: Customer Loyalty Programmes
    SIC 31: Revenue-Barter Transactions involving the legal form of a lease
Companies Income Tax Act Cap C21 2004 LFN
Value Added Tax Act Cap V1 2004 LFN
Midaspage, Nigeria (2012) Tax Consequences of Adopting IFRS in Nigeria

# IAS 11 Construction Contracts

## 6.1 Introduction

A construction contract is defined in IAS 11 as a contract specifically negotiated for the construction of an asset or a combination of assets that are closely interrelated or interdependent in terms of their design, technology and function or their ultimate purpose or use.

The key issue in accounting for construction contracts is the allocation of contract revenue and costs to relevant accounting periods as construction work usually span across several financial years.

The scope of IAS 11 covers contracts for construction of single assets as well as assets that are closely related or interdependent. Construction contracts may include:

- Contracts for the destruction or restoration of assets and restoration of the environment following the demolition of assets.
- Contracts for rendering services directly related to the construction of the asset; the services of architects or project managers are some examples.
- Contract to supply a large piece of a production plant.

## 6.2 Classification of contracts

Two types of contract are identified in the standard:

**a. Fixed-price contract**:  Is a construction contract in which the contractor agrees to a fixed contract price or a fixed rate per unit of output, which in some cases is subjected to cost escalation clauses.

**b**. **Cost-plus contract:** Is a construction contract in which the contractor is reimbursed for allowable or otherwise defined costs, plus a percentage of these costs or a fixed fee.

Though most construction contracts span across more than one accounting period, some contracts may be concluded within an accounting period and are also covered within the scope of IAS 11. This means there is no fixed contractual period stated in the definition of a construction contract.

### 6.3 Determination of Contract Cost and Revenue

The following will constitute the cost to and revenue from a construction contract:

**Cost:** Contract costs comprise:
- Cost that relates directly to the specific contract such as: cost of materials, site labour, depreciation of plant and equipment, transportation cost for moving materials and equipments to and from contract site, claims from third parties etc.
- Cost of activities attributable to and allocated to specific contracts such as, insurance, construction overheads etc.
- Cost specifically chargeable to the client in the contract agreement, administrative cost for example.

**Revenue:** Contract revenue comprises:
- The initial agreed total contract price
- Additional variations price, claims and incentive payments.

### Scenario 6.1: Profit on contract using percentage of completion

HydroConstruct Ltd has been awarded three years contract for N150million. The estimated cost of completion is N95million. At the end of the first year HydroConstruct has incurred costs of N43.7million and a progress payment of N70million has been received. Evaluate the financial statement and tax effects.

In the first year, the contract is 46% completed (N43.7million of N95million) using the percentage of completion method to determine the stage of completion. Revenue in year 1 would be N69million (46% of N150million). N1million (N70million less N69million) will be recognized as deferred income in the statement of financial position. Corporation tax of 32% would be paid on the profit attributable to the stage of completion in the first year. The VAT payable will be N3.5million (5% of N70million).

## 6.4 Recognition and Measurement

Contract revenue is measured at the fair value of the consideration received or receivable. The recognition would depend on the following:

*   Where the outcome of a contract can be reliably estimated, contract costs and revenue are recognized based on the stage of completion of the contract activity at the reporting date. The stage of completion is determined by reference to portion of cost incurred in relation to estimated total cost, surveys of work performed and the physical proportion of the contract.

*   Where the outcome of a contract cannot be reliably estimated, contract costs are recognized as expense when incurred and revenue is recognized to the extent that recovery of contract cost is probable

*   Where it is probable that contract costs will exceed total contract revenue, the expected loss should be recognized immediately as an expense.

### Scenario 6.2: Loss on Contract

StevStructures has been awarded a 3-year construction contract. Based on percentage of completion, N1.2million profit was recognized in the first year. In the second year, facts available to management are that the contract will incur a loss of N2.7million. Evaluate financial statement and tax effects.

The initial projections revealed that the contract was profitable hence the recognition of N1.2million profit in year 1. With the new facts available, StveSturcture management must recognize a total loss of N3.9million (N1.2million plus N2.7million) in the second year financial statement. Prior-period adjustment would not be appropriate, and the loss is not as a result of the inability to recover payment for work done rather it is a revision of the estimated cost to complete the contract.

Corporation tax of N384,000.00 (32% of N1.2million) would have been paid on this contract in the first year tax returns. In the second year, the loss of N3.9million could be used to offset the income from other contracts to arrive at the total profit of the second year. Where the loss of N3.9million results to a total loss, the unrelieved loss can be carried forward and relieved against subsequent year's profit. VAT is charged on the contract price and payable when payments are received.

## 6.5 Tax Implications

### Income tax and Education Tax
Profits and gains from each contract will be subject to tax in line with the provisions of the Companies Income Tax Act and Education Tax Act. Losses incurred from separate contracts can be relieved against profit from other contracts. This means the assessable profit in any tax year shall be the aggregation of profits and losses from all contracts carried out by the entity.

Where a loss is recognized in a particular contract due to non-payment by the client, the revenue would require objective evidence to proof that the debt is impaired and the amount is not collectible.

### Value added tax
Construction contracts are taxable supplies and therefore VATable. This means the VAT payable is determined on the total contract price agreed. However, VAT is charged at the stage of completion of the contract and based on the amount invoiced to client.

Contracts involving purchase of materials and equipment will give arise to off-settable input VAT claimable by the contractor.

**Withholding Tax**
Where a contractor hires a sub-contractor, tax is required to be deducted at source from payment made to the sub-contractor.

**Mobilization Payment**
Based on the timing difference between when revenue is deemed to have been earned and recognized in accounts and cash flow received from construction contracts, reconciliation will be required to ascertain the correct amount to be reported in the profit or loss statement as revenue from contracts for VAT and income and education tax purposes. For example:

In any accounting period where cash received is lower than the amount recognized as revenue for period, based on the stage of completion of the contract would give rise to the challenge of payment of VAT on amount earned but not yet received. The outstanding amount should be reported as contract revenue receivable in the statement of financial position and the VAT will be paid in the accounting period payment is received.

Where payment received is higher than the actual contract work done at the reporting date will result to remittance of VAT on revenue not yet earned. The unrealized revenue will be reported as deferred income in statement of financial position and to be released to the profit or loss statement in subsequent accounting period.

## References

IFRS RED Book 2012 PART A: 'the conceptual framework and requirements' and PART B: 'the accompanying documents'
  IAS 11: Construction Contracts
  IFRIC 12 Service Concession Arrangements
Companies Income Tax Act Cap C21 2004 LFN
Midaspage, Nigeria (2010) Tax Consequences of Adopting IFRS in Nigeria

# IAS 16: Property, Plant and Equipment

## 7.1 Introduction

IAS 16 defines Property, Plant and Equipment (PPE) as tangible items that:
- Are held for use in the production or supply of goods or services, for rental to others, or for administrative purposes; and
- Are expected to be used during more than one accounting period.

IAS 16 requires that non-current assets are initially recorded at cost and included in the financial statements at their carrying value.

Cost is defined as '...the amount of cash or cash equivalents paid or the fair value of the other consideration given to acquire an asset at the time of its acquisition or construction'.

Carrying value is defined as '...the amount at which an asset is recognized after deducting any accumulated depreciation and any accumulated impairment losses...'

## 7.2 Recognition and Measurement

Initial Recognition: A tangible non-current asset is initially recorded at cost. This may include:
- Purchase price after any trade discounts (but before settlement discounts)
- Transport and handling costs
- Non-refundable tax such as import duties
- Site preparation

- Installation costs
- Professional fees such as legal costs
- If the asset is self-constructed, labour costs of the entity's own employees
- Borrowing cost
- Future dismantling and restoration cost

Future dismantling and restoration costs are included as part of the cost of a non-current asset only where these costs are recorded as a provision under IAS 37. Any abnormal costs such as wastage and costs arising from errors do not form part of the cost of the asset, and must be expensed as incurred.

**Subsequent costs:** Subsequent expenditure on a non-current asset may be capitalized where:
a. The expenditure enhances the economic benefits of the asset in excess of its current standard of performance. This may be through:
- Extension of the asset's life
- Increase in production capacity
- Improved quality of output

Any other expenditure including repairs must be expensed to the profit or loss statement in the period in which it is incurred.

### 7.3 Revaluation of tangible non-current assets

IAS 16 allows non-current assets to be measured using either the cost model or the revaluation model. The standard requires that where the revaluation model is applied:
- It is applied consistently to all assets of the same class of PPE and
- Assets are revalued sufficiently regularly that their carrying amount is not significantly different from their fair value.

**Upward revaluation:** Where an asset is revalued upwards, this is accounted for by:
- Dr: Non-Current Asset with the difference between cost and revalued amount

- Dr: Accumulated depreciation with all depreciation on the revalued asset to date
- Cr: Other comprehensive income (revaluation surplus) with the difference between valuation and previous carrying value

**Downwards revaluation:** Where an asset is revalued downwards, the accounting entries depend on whether the asset has previously been revalued upwards:

a. *Not previously revalued upwards*
- Dr: Profit or Loss statement
- Cr: Non-current asset

b. *Previously revalued upwards*
Dr: Other comprehensive income (to the extent revaluation surplus was previously credited)
- Dr: Profit or Loss statement
- Cr: Non-current asset

**Reversal of downwards revaluation**
- Dr: Non-current asset
- Cr: Profit or Loss Statement (to the extent revaluation surplus was previously charged)
- Cr: Other comprehensive income

**Depreciation of a revalued asset:** Depreciation is charged on a revalued asset as normal, based on a depreciable amount of valuation less residual value spread over the remaining useful life.

Depreciation is charged to the profit or loss statement but a reserves transfer may be made to transfer the difference between the actual depreciation charge and the historical cost depreciation charge from the revaluation reserve to retained earnings:
- Dr: Revaluation reserve with excess depreciation
- Cr: Retained earnings with excess depreciation

## 7.4 Non-depreciable assets and componentization

The standard permits the use of judgment to identify the extent to which items of Property, Plant and Equipment shall be aggregated and treated as single asset and where a large item should be broken into significant component parts. The significant component parts may be treated as separate depreciable assets possessing different useful lives.

Land and buildings are separable assets and are accounted for separately, even when they are acquired together. Land has unlimited useful life and therefore is not depreciated. In some cases where the useful life of land is limited (quarries and landfill sites), it is depreciated in the manner that reflects the benefits to be derived from it.

Buildings have limited useful life therefore are depreciable assets. Any increase in the value of land on which a building stands does not affect the determination of the depreciable amount of the building.

Any part of an item of Property, Plant and Equipment with a cost that is significant in relation to the total cost of the item should be depreciated separately. Examples of such assets include a blast furnace with lining, an aircraft with its engines and seats, oil rig with hoisting systems, mud system etc having different useful lives.

## 7.5 Disposal of tangible non-current assets

The gain or loss on disposal of a non-current asset is calculated as the difference between proceeds and the asset's carrying value on the date of disposal. This applies to assets held under both the cost and revaluation models. Any resulting gain or loss on disposal is recognized in the profit or loss statement.

Where a previously revalued asset is disposed of, any balance remaining in the revaluation reserve relating to this asset is transferred to retained earnings and disclosed in the statement of changes in equity.

## 7.6 Borrowing Costs

IAS 23 requires that borrowing cost associated with the acquisition, construction or production of a qualifying asset be capitalized as part of the cost of that asset.

Borrowing costs are defined as interest and other costs that an entity incurs in connection with the borrowing of funds. A qualifying asset is defined as an asset that necessarily takes a substantial period of time to get ready for its intended use or sale.

**Eligible Borrowing Costs:** Where an entity borrows money specifically to acquire or construct a qualifying asset, all of the actual borrowing costs incurred, less any income from the temporary investment of the money borrowed, must be capitalized.

Where money is borrowed centrally from a number of sources, and to fund a number of projects, the borrowing costs to be capitalized as part of the cost of a non-current asset must be calculated based on the weighted average cost of general borrowings.

### Scenario 7.1: Borrowing cost capitalized

Poshbank borrowed N5billion specifically to finance the cost of constructing its new office. The tenor of the loan is 15months and the interest rate is 12% per annum. The construction of the building was completed within 11 months. As the management envisaged the reduction in the period of construction, it temporary reinvested a portion of the money borrowed at rate of 15% to earn a total interest of N120million within 9months of the tenor of the original loan. Evaluate financial statement and tax effects.

The amount to be capitalized as cost of the new head office is N5.49billion (N5billion plus N550million less N60million). The amount to be capitalized is the principal amount borrowed and the interest accrued for the period of construction less any interest earn on temporary investment of the money borrowed. The total interest payable on the loan borrowed was N750million (12% of N5billion*15/12).

The amount on which capital allowance is claimable is N5billion. The net interest of N630million is a revenue expenditure and tax deductible.

**Period of Capitalization**: The capitalization of borrowing costs commences when:
- Expenditure on the asset has commenced;
- Borrowing costs are being incurred;
- Activities necessary to prepare the asset for its intended use are in progress

Capitalization of borrowing cost will be suspended during an extended period where development process is interrupted, due to industrial action or delay in the supply chain except where the delay is part of the development process.

Capitalization of borrowing costs ceases when substantially all the activities necessary to prepare the qualifying asset for its intended use or sale are completed.

### 7.7 Tax Implications

**Capital Allowance**

Non-current assets are referred to as qualifying capital expenditures for income tax purpose. In the computation of tax liability, capital allowance is to be deducted to arrive at the total profit before applying the tax rate. Capital allowance is granted to replace depreciation charge disallowed in the determination of assessable/adjusted profit.

The Revenue usually requires acceptance certificate issued by the Federal Ministry of Commerce and Industries as proof that the non-current assets were acquired and are in use for the purpose of the business of the entity.

Where an entity obtains a loan to finance the acquisition of non-current asset, for the purpose of capital allowance, only the initial cost incurred or principal amount to acquire the asset will be relevant. The subsequent finance cost or interest should be treated as revenue expenditure therefore deductible for income tax purpose.

Where an entity adopts the revaluation model to account for non-current asset, the increase arising from revaluation is to be credited other comprehensive income. For the purpose of capital allowance, the revaluation surplus/deficit will not be taken into consideration. Also any amount charged or credited to profit or loss statement as a result of adjustments for revaluation should be disregarded.

**Disposal of Assets**
Where non-current assets are disposed off, for tax purposes, the entity is required to carry out balancing adjustment. This could result to balancing allowance, balancing charge and Capital Gain.

On the date of disposal, if the sales proceed is less than the tax written down value (TWDV) of the asset, the entity will be entitled to balancing allowance claim which will be deducted from assessable profit of the year of assessment the asset was disposed.

Where the sales proceed is greater than the tax written down value of the asset on the date of disposal, the entity will be deemed to have earned an income called balancing charge which is liable to tax. The balancing charge would be restricted to the total capital allowance previously claimed on the asset. The excess of the sales proceed over the total capital allowance previously claimed on the asset is treated as Capital Gain which is liable to tax under the Capital Gains Tax Act Cap C1 2004 LFN.

In determining assessable profit, gains or profit on sale of assets is not taxable while the loss from disposal is not tax deductible.

The proceeds from disposal of non-current asset is a taxable supply liable to VAT at the current rate of 5%.

## Deferred Tax

Deferred Tax is the tax effect on temporary differences. Temporary differences are the differences between the carrying value of assets in the statement of financial position and the tax base of the assets at the reporting date.

The differences in rates applicable for the computation of depreciation and capital allowance will give rise to differences between the carrying values and the tax base of the assets. The deferred tax could be an asset or a liability to be reported in the statement of financial position. The movements from one year to another in the deferred tax account would represent a charge or abatement in the profit or loss statement.

### References
IFRS RED Book 2012 PART A: 'the conceptual framework and requirements' and PART B: 'the accompanying documents'
    IAS 16 Property, Plant and Equipment
    IAS 23 Borrowing Costs
Companies Income Tax Act Cap C21 2004 LFN
Value Added Tax Act Cap V1 2004 LFN
Midaspage, Nigeria (2010) Tax Consequences of Adopting IFRS in Nigeria

# IAS 40: Investment Property

## 8.1 Introduction

IAS 40 defines Investment property as a property (land or a building – or part of a building – or both) held to earn rental or for capital appreciation or for both rather than for:
a. Use in the production or supply of goods or services or for administrative purpose or
b. Sale in the ordinary course of business.

The scope of IAS 40 includes the following:
* Land held for a currently undetermined future use;
* A building leased out under an operating lease
* Land held for long term in order to benefit from an increase in market value
* Property under construction to be used in future to earn rental or capital appreciation

The following properties would not qualify as investment property under IAS 40:
* Property intended for sale in the ordinary course of business
* Property being constructed or developed on behalf of third parties, example, a owner-occupied property
* Property leased to another entity under a finance lease

## 8.2 Accounting for Investment Properties

In effect, acquiring investment properties is an alternative way for a company to utilize surplus cash to earn returns rather than putting it in a bank or using it to purchase stocks and shares. These properties are not used by the business, but rather held to generate income and long term capital growth.

It therefore follows that the accounting treatment for non-current assets is not necessarily applicable to investment properties. In particular, there is little need to depreciate such assets when they are held especially for long-term capital appreciation.

### Scenario 8.1: Accounting for investment properties

Due to the economic down turn and the slump in the stock market, Excel Securities decided to invest its surplus cash in acquiring a plot of land, a hall and an office complex. Excel Securities may use the land to build its new head office in the future or sell it to realize huge profit if the prices of properties soar in the nearest future. The hall is being used as an event centre and available to the public. The office complex is leased to various companies for their businesses.

In the first year of acquiring the properties, it was realized that the market value of the land has increased slightly and the office complex has fallen marginally by 10% and 6% respectively. The hall enjoyed considerable patronage from the public. Evaluate financial statement and tax effects.

Within the scope of IAS 40, land held for undetermined future use and buildings leased out under operating lease to earn rentals income or for capital appreciation qualify as investment properties. The initial recognition of the properties would be at cost. Subsequently, Excel Securities has the option to adopt either the cost model or fair value model. The company would have to apply consistently whichever model it chooses to all the three investment properties.

If the cost model is applied, the properties would be reported in financial statement at cost less depreciation less impairment loss at each reporting date. For tax purpose, depreciation and impairment loss charge to profit or loss statement will not be tax deductible. The hall and the office complex will be entitled to capital allowance claim. Deferred tax will be determined accordingly at each reporting date. When the properties are disposed off, Excel Securities would be required to carry out balancing adjustment which may result to either balancing allowance or balancing charge and capital gain.

If fair value model is applied, the market value of the properties would be the point of reference to ascertain either a gain or loss in fair value. In this case, a gain of 10% would be reported on the land while a loss of 6% would be reported on the office complex accordingly. The properties would not be depreciated. If the fair value gain is treated as unrealized gain and exempted from tax, the fair value loss will not be tax deductible. Conversely, if fair value gains are taxable the losses would be tax deductible. Disposal of investment properties would be regarded as capital gain.

Rental incomes are taxable supplies liable to VAT. The rents received from event centre and office complex would attract VAT. Note that the office complex is being used for commercial purpose. The lessees (office tenants) are required to withhold tax at source from lease rental. The rentals from event centre may not attract VAT because the hirers may not be taxable persons.

## 8.3 Recognition and Measurement

Investment property shall be recognized as an asset when:
It is probable that the future economic benefits that are associated with the investment property will flow to the entity; and
The cost of the investment property can be measured reliably

IAS 40 requires that investment properties are initially measured at cost. The cost should comprise the purchase price and any directly attributable expenditure. Direct attributable expenditure includes professional fees for legal services, property transfer taxes and other transaction costs.

For subsequent measurement, the standard permits an entity to adopt either the fair value model or the cost model as its accounting policy and to apply that policy to all of its investment property.

**Cost model:** Investment properties accounted for using the cost model are held in accordance with IAS 16 that is at cost less depreciation less impairment losses. These properties cannot be revalued.

**Fair value model:** In this case, the property is measured to fair value each year. This is normally established by reference to the market price of the asset. Any change in fair value since the last measurement date is recognized in the profit or loss statement. Properties held under the fair value model are not depreciated.

### 8.4 Transfer and Disposal of Investment Property

**a. Transfer:** There is a transfer to or from investment property in the change of use evidenced by:

- *Owner-occupation and investment property*: There is a transfer from investment property to owner-occupation on commencement of owner-occupation and transfer back to investment property when the owner ceased to occupy the property for investment purpose.

- *Investment property and Inventory*: There is a transfer from investment property to inventory on commencement of development with the intention to sell the property. It moves from inventory to investment property on commencement of an operating lease to a third party.

**b. Disposal:** An investment property is derecognized from the statement of financial position on the sale or permanent withdrawal of the property from use and no further economic benefits are expected from its disposal.

Gains and losses from the disposal of the investment property are to be recognized in the profit or loss statement as the difference between the net disposal proceeds and the carrying amount or as otherwise treated in a lease arrangement under IAS 17.

## 8.5 Tax Implications

Investment Properties are accounted for using either cost or fair value model.

**Cost Model:** The property is to be depreciated and tested for impairment annually. For income tax purposes, depreciation charge and any impairment loss will not be tax deductible. However, the reporting entity can claim capital allowance on the investment property accordingly.

When the investment is disposed off, balancing adjustment will be computed and proceed from the sale is VATable.

**Fair value:** The property will not be depreciated rather changes in fair value will be recognized in the profit or loss statement. Gains or losses from fair value adjustment are treated as non-taxable and non-deductible respectively for income tax purpose.

On disposal of the investment property, the gain from disposal is a capital gain liable to tax under the Capital Gains Tax Act Cap C1 2004 LFN. It is important to posit that if the entity's business is construction, acquisition and disposal of properties, the sale of property would be acting in the ordinary course of business and such gains or profits would be liable to income tax.

**Rental Income:** Where the investment property is leased or rented out, the consideration earned will be liable to income tax. Rental incomes are taxable supplies especially where the transaction is between two entities and the investment property will be deployed for commercial purpose by the tenant or the lessee. Payment of rent will also attract tax deduction at source.

## References

IFRS RED Book 2012 PART A: 'the conceptual framework and requirements' and PART B: 'the accompanying documents'

    IAS 40 Investment Property

Companies Income Tax Act Cap C21 2004 LFN

Value Added Tax Act Cap V1 2004 LFN

Midaspage, Nigeria (2010) Tax Consequences of Adopting IFRS in Nigeria

# IFRS 5: Non-Current Assets Held For Sale and Discontinued Operations

## 9.1 Introduction

IFRS 5 applies to assets or disposal groups for which the carrying value will be recovered primarily through sale rather than through continuing use. This includes the planned sale of an interest in a subsidiary that would lead to loss of control even if some shares are retained. A disposal group may be a group of cash-generating units, a single cash generating unit, or part of cash generating units consisting of non-current and current assets and liabilities excluding:

- Deferred tax assets
- Assets arising from employees' benefits
- Financial assets within the scope of IFRS 9
- Contractual rights under insurance contracts
- Biological assets under IAS 41

## 9.2 Conditions for Classification

An asset will be moved from non-current assets to current assets and classified as *held for sale* if it fulfils certain criteria as follows:

- Sell: The management or directors are committed and intended to sell the asset at year end.
- Available: The related asset must be available for disposal
- Locate: The directors must be actively seeking to locate a potential buyer at the year end.
- Expected: The sale is highly probable and expected to be completed within 12 months from year end.

## Scenario 9.1: Disposal not classified as held for sale

As a result of the downturn in the economy during the accounting period ended 31st December 2009, JPMoola Ltd decided to maintain its Plant in workable condition and cease deploying the assets pending when economic conditions will improve. The plant currently has a carrying value of N13.5million. JPMoola Ltd subsequently disposed of the asset within three months after the year end for N12million. Evaluate financial statement and tax effects.

JPMoola, would not be required to classify the plant as 'held for sale' as at year ended 31st December 2009 because JPMoola directors did not intend to sell the asset but keep it until when it is profitable for the asset to be redeployed. Though the sale occurred within 12 months after year end it was not expected at the year end.

Though the use of the asset was suspended, depreciation will be charged up to the disposal date. It however appeared that the asset has been impaired since its carrying value is greater than the sales price.

The depreciation charge and the impairment loss would not be tax deductible, but JPMoola would be entitled to capital allowance claim up to 31st December 2009. Balancing adjustment would be carried out in the 2011 tax year tax returns based on the accounts for the year ended 31st December 2010 accordingly. Disposal of non-current assets are taxable supplies liable to VAT at the rate of 5%.

### 9.3 Recognition and Measurement

Non-current asset or disposal group should be classified as *held for sale* if its carrying value will be recovered principally through a sale transaction rather than through continuing use.

**Initial recognition:** Once an asset fulfils the conditions as held for sale the following would apply:

- Non-current assets classified as held for sale are not depreciated.
- The asset is classified as such and presented immediately before total assets, as part of current assets on the statement of financial position.
- It is measured at the lower of carrying amount and fair value less cost to sell.
- Where fair value less cost to sell is lower than carrying value, an impairment loss is recognized in the profit or loss statement
- Where the asset is measured under the revaluation model in IAS 16, it must be revalued immediately prior to being classified as *held for sale*. This makes the carrying amount equal to fair value and means that on classification as *held for sale*, an impairment charge equal to the costs to sell is recognized.

**Subsequent Measurement**

If non-current assets *held for sale* are not sold within 12 months of their classification, they may remain classified as *held for sale* provided that:
- The delay to the sale was outside the selling entity's control; and
- The entity is still committed to the sale plan
- If the criteria to be held for sale are no longer met, the asset must cease to be classified as *held for sale* and is returned to non-current asset at the lower of:
  i. Its carrying value had it never been classified as *held for sale*
  ii. Its recoverable amount when the *held for sale* criteria ceased to be met

**Scenario 9.2: Disposal qualified as held for sale**

The facts are the same as in case 12.1. On 2nd August 2009, JPMoola decided that the plant should be sold. It instructed an agent to locate a willing party that will buy the assets at any price close to its carrying value. The agent would charge a fee of 5% of the sales price. Evaluate financial statement and tax effects.

The plant should be classified as *held for sale* in the year ended 31st December 2009 as it met the criteria because the sale was highly probable by the instruction of the agent to sell the plant and the sale took place within 12 months after the reporting date.

JPMoola, will stop depreciating the assets immediately the decision to sell was reached and the asset should be classified as *held for sale* under current asset in the statement of financial position at year end.

The asset will be deemed to have been disposed off during the period ending 31st December 2009 and will not be entitled to capital allowance claim. Balancing adjustment will be computed in the 2010 tax year tax returns for the sale proceed being nil. This means the applicable tax effect is deferred until when cash is realized.

### 9.4 Tax implications

The tax law has provided that qualifying capital expenditures shall be entitled to capital allowance claim and where there is a disposal, the tax payer should determine balancing adjustments. Non-current assets classified as *held for sale* would give rise to the following tax implications:

- The meaning of disposal for tax purpose is not restricted to only when an asset is sold but includes when the asset is no-longer used by the business, stolen, expiration of a concession or a lease period.
- Technically, when an entity moves its assets previously classified as non-current or fixed assets to any other form or write-off would suggest a disposal.
- Assets classified as held-for-sale are not to be depreciated and thus for tax purpose, the entity cannot claim capital allowance on the asset for the same period.
- Impairment test is to be carried out on non-current assets classified as held for sale. Impairment loss recognized in the profit

or loss statement will not be allowed for income tax purpose. This will also impact on the deferred tax account of the entity.

- Where the asset is reclassified to non-current assets, capital allowance will be computed on the TWDV when capital allowance was suspended.

### References

IFRS RED Book 2012 PART A: 'the conceptual framework and requirements' and PART B: 'the accompanying documents'

IFRS 5 Non-current Assets Held for Sale and Discontinued Operations

Companies Income Tax Act Cap C21 2004 LFN

Midaspage, Nigeria (2010) Tax Consequences of Adopting IFRS in Nigeria

# IAS 38: Intangible Assets

## 10.1 Introduction

An intangible asset is an <u>identifiable</u> non-monetary asset without physical substance <u>controlled</u> as a result of past event and from which future <u>economic benefits</u> are expected to flow to the entity. Examples of intangible assets include:
- Computer software
- Patents, copyrights
- Motion picture films
- Customer lists
- Franchises
- Fishing right

IAS 38 applies to all intangible assets except those specifically covered in other accounting standards such as: deferred tax assets, inventory, leases, insurance contracts, financial assets, assets arising from employee benefits, mineral rights and exploration and evaluation cost of minerals and goodwill acquired in a business combination.

## 10.2 Criteria for recognition

An item should not be recognized as an intangible asset unless it fully meets the definition in the standard.

*i. Identifiable* – the transfer of a legal right through purchase or could be sold separately.
*ii. Control* – legally enforce right over the asset and prevent the access of others.

- Legal right over technical knowledge or know-how
- The skills of employees as a result of training cost incurred cannot be recognized
- Market share and customer loyalty cannot be recognized

***iii. Economic Benefits*** – from sale of the product/service or a reduction in expenditure/cost savings.

The cost of an intangible asset is recognized if and only if both the following occur:
- It is probable that the future economic benefits that are attributable to the asset will flow to the entity.
- The cost can be measured reliably.

All expenditure related to an intangible asset which does not meet the criteria for recognition must be expensed. Examples include:
- Start up cost
- Advertising costs
- Training cost
- Business relocation cost
- Prepaid costs for services such as advertising or marketing costs for campaigns that have not been launched can be recognized as prepayment.

Other **internally generated intangible assets** such as own brands, customer lists, publishing titles etc do not qualify for recognition.

### 10.3 Research and Development Cost

**Research costs** comprise the following:
- Activities aimed at obtaining new knowledge
- The search for, evaluation and final selection of, applications of research findings or other knowledge
- The search for alternative for materials, devices, products, processes, systems or services
- The formulation, design evaluation and final selection of possible alternatives for new or improved materials, device, products, system or services

Costs incurred at the research stage of a project are written off as expense because it cannot be certain that future economic benefits will probably flow to the entity from the project.

**Development costs** are incurred at a later stage in a project, and the probability of success should be more apparent. Such costs include:
- The design, construction and testing of pre-production or pre-use prototypes and models
- The design of tools, jigs, moulds and dies involving new technology
- The design, construction and operation of a pilot plant that is not of a scale economically feasible for commercial production
- The design, construction and testing of a chosen alternative for new or improved materials, devices, products, processes, systems or services

Development costs are recognized if they meet the following criteria:
- The technical feasibility of completing the intangible asset so that it will be available for use or sale.
- Its intention to complete the intangible asset and use or sell it
- Its ability to use or sell the intangible asset
- Its ability to measure the expenditure attributable to the intangible asset during its development reliably
- How the intangible asset will generate probable future economic benefits. Among other things, the entity should demonstrate the existence of a market for the output of the intangible asset or the intangible asset itself or, if it is to be used internally, the usefulness of the intangible asset.

## 10.4 Recognition and Measurement

Intangible assets are measured initially at cost, but subsequently can be carried at cost or revalued amount.

*Cost Model*: Under the cost model, intangible assets are carried at cost less any accumulated amortization and less any accumulated impairment losses.

**Revaluation model**: Intangible assets are to be carried at fair value at the revaluation date less any subsequent accumulated amortization and impairment losses.
- Fair value with reference to active market
- The entire class must be revalued
- If there is no active market, the asset should be carried at cost less any accumulated amortization and any impairment loss.
- Revaluation carried regularly
- Upward revaluation are charges to revaluation surplus while downward revaluation are charged to profit or loss statement

### 10.5 Useful life

The useful life of an intangible asset may be finite or indefinite. An indefinite useful life suggests that there is no foreseeable limit to the period over which the asset is expected to generate net cash inflows for the entity.

**Finite**: intangible assets with finite useful life should be:
- Amortized over its useful life
- Amortization starts when the asset is available for use
- Amortization ceases when the asset is classified as held-for-sale or derecognized
- Amortization should reflect the pattern in which the future economic benefits from the assets is consumed
- Amortized amount charged to statement of profit or loss

**Indefinite**: Intangible assets with indefinite useful life is not amortized but tested annually for impairment. Indefinite useful life means that there is no foreseeable limit on the period of time the asset will contribute cash flows to the entity. Indefinite is not the same as infinite that is limitless in extent.

Intangible asset should be eliminated from statement of financial position and gain or loss recognized in the profit or loss when it is disposed off or when no further economic benefit is expected from its future use.

## Scenario 10.1 Accounting for Intangible Asset

iSports TV has acquired the broadcasting right of 'mankind most followed sport' for seven years. iSports TV intends to renew and retain the right before it expires and there is no factor suggesting that the broadcasting right will not be renewed. Evaluate Financial Statement and Tax Effects.

The broadcasting right or license is an intangible asset. The license is identifiable, legally enforceable and would generate cash flow to iSports TV. The license will be treated as asset with indefinite useful life since the entity intends to renew and it is certain that the license will be renewed. The intangible asset will not be amortized but test for impairment annually.

In the event that, the renewal is uncertain due to any decision to auction the broadcasting right to the public rather an automatic renewal for iSports TV, the intangible asset will be amortized over the useful life.

The cash flows generated from the broadcasting right is taxable and iSports TV is earning the income because it acquires the license. The license is not a qualifying capital expenditure on which capital allowance is granted. For income tax purposes, the cost of the intangible asset should be an allowable expense whether the intangible asset has finite or indefinite useful life. A temporary difference may arise if different treatment is given for accounting and tax purposes.

### 10.6 Goodwill

IFRS 3 defines goodwill as an intangible asset acquired in a business combination representing the future economic benefits arising from assets that are not capable of being individually identified and separately recognized. It means the value of the business as a going concern is greater than the value of its separate tangible assets.

Purchased goodwill arising on consolidation is retained in the statement of financial position because it has been paid for; it has no tangible substance hence recognized as intangible non-current asset. Goodwill and other intangible assets acquired are to be accounted for as follows:

- Goodwill acquired in a business combination is initially measured at cost, subsequently at cost less any accumulated impairment losses.
- Acquired goodwill is not amortized, but must be reviewed annually for impairment.
- The fair value of intangible assets acquired in business combination can normally be measured with sufficient reliability to be recognized separately from goodwill.

### 10.7 Tax Implications

### Capital Allowance

The amount representing the cost of intangible asset may be a qualifying capital expenditure for capital allowance purpose. Examples include qualifying research and development expenditure and qualifying plant and equipment expenditure.

For the purpose of taxation, plant and machinery is defined to include whatever apparatus actively used for the purpose of trade. Capital expenditures on computer software comprising programs and data will be qualifying capital expenditure for which capital allowance is claimable.

Entities engaged in research and development activities for commercialization are allowed 20% investment tax credit on their qualifying expenditure.

### Income Tax

Cost of intangible assets referred to as preliminary expenses, formation expenses or deferred charges which were usually amortized over a period of sixty months depending on the company's accounting policies do meet the recognition criteria of intangible assets under IAS 38. Such costs are to be written off to profit or loss statement and would not be deductible in the ascertainment of assessable profit.

Provision for research and development is allowed subject to a cap of 10% of the total profit in that year of assessment.

Where the cost representing intangible asset is not regarded as a qualifying capital expenditure, the annual amortization of the cost of intangible asset or the impairment loss of an intangible asset with an indefinite useful life should be treated as an allowable deduction for income tax purpose.

Surplus or loss arising from revaluing intangible assets are to be adjusted for and recognized in the appropriate sections of the Statement of Profit or Loss and Other Comprehensive Income.

**Deferred Tax**

The systematic allocation of the depreciable amount of an intangible asset may be different from the treatment accorded to the intangible asset for tax purpose. This will give rise to a temporary difference and a deferred tax asset or liability should be recognized in the financial statement. The measurement of deferred tax will depend on whether the intangible asset has finite or indefinite useful life and whether the recovery of the carrying value of the intangible asset will be through sale or continuous use.

**References**

IFRS RED Book 2012 PART A: 'the conceptual framework and requirements' and PART B: 'the accompanying documents'

    IAS 38 Intangible Assets

    IFRS 3 Business Combinations

Companies Income Tax Act Cap C21 2004 LFN

Midaspage Tax & IFRS Academy (2012) IFRS: Tax Implications

# IAS 36: Impairment of Assets

## 11.1 Introduction

IAS 36 Impairment of assets requires annual impairment tests for certain assets and for any non-financial asset where there is an indication of impairment.

The objective is to ensure that assets are not overstated in the statement of financial position. That is, an entity's assets should be carried at no more than their recoverable amount. Specifically:
- Non-current assets and goodwill are recorded in the financial statements at no more than their recoverable amount
- Any resulting impairment loss is measured and recognized on a consistent basis
- Sufficient information is disclosed in the financial statements to enable users to understand the impact of the impairment on the financial statements of the reporting entity.

The scope of IAS 36 covers non-current assets as well as cash generating units (CGU) and applies to subsidiaries, associates and joint ventures that are accounted for at cost in the investing entity's separate financial statements under:
- IAS 27 Consolidated and separate financial statements
- IAS 28 Investments in associates
- IAS 31 Interest in Joint Ventures

IAS 36 specifically excludes the following from its scope:
- Inventories
- Assets arising from construction contracts
- Deferred tax assets
- Financial assets within the scope of IAS 39
- Investment property measured at fair value

IAS 36 also applies to some assets carried at a revalued amount under other IFRS, such as the revaluation model in IAS 16. Where the revalued asset's fair value is based on market value, the only difference between that revalued amount and fair value less cost to sell will be the direct incremental cost of disposing off the asset.

## 11.2 Use of Judgments and Estimates

The judgments and estimates involved in making impairment calculations are stated in IAS 1 and explicitly captured in IAS 36.

IAS 1 requires disclosure of the judgments that management has used in applying the entity's significant accounting policies. IAS 1 also requires disclosure of the key assumptions concerning the future and other key sources of estimation and uncertainty at the balance sheet date, that have a significant risk of causing a material adjustment to the carrying amount of assets and liabilities within the next financial year.

## 11.3 Impairment test

An impairment test will involve calculating recoverable amount for comparison with carrying amount as follows:
- Check whether impairment has occurred
- If carrying amount is greater than recoverable amount, it means asset has impaired
- If recoverable amount is greater than carrying amount, it means no impairment
- The recoverable amount is the higher of fair value less costs to sell and value in use
- Value in use is the present value of future cash flows generated by asset

**Carrying Amount:** An asset's carrying amount is the amount at which the asset is recognized after deducting any accumulated depreciation or amortization and accumulated impairment losses thereon.

**Recoverable Amount:** Recoverable amount is the higher of the amounts to be realized through the asset's use or sale. An asset's recoverable amount represents its greatest value to the business in terms of cash flows that it can generate. Simply put, it is the higher of fair value less costs to sell and value in use.

a. *Fair Value less Cost to Sell:* is the amount obtainable from the sale of an asset in an arm's length transaction between knowledgeable, willing parties less the costs of disposal.
b. *Value in Use:* is the present value of the future cash flows expected to be generated by an asset, including its ultimate disposal

- Future cash flows should be based on the most recent budgets and are generally for a maximum of five years.
- The discount rate used should be a pre-tax rate reflecting current assessments of the time value of money.

Both fair value less cost to sell and value in use can be difficult to determine in practice. It may be possible to determine fair value less cost to sell even if an asset is not traded in an active market. Sometimes it will not be possible to make an estimate of fair value less costs to sell as there is no basis for making a reliable estimate. In such circumstances, recoverable amount should be determined by estimating the asset's value in use.

Estimating value in use is a matter of judgment, not fact, requiring estimates of cash flows many years into the future and determining appropriate discount rates to bring them back to their present values. The objective is to make estimates as realistic as possible.

It is not always necessary to calculate both measures when performing an impairment review. If an asset's fair value less cost to sell or its value in use exceeds the asset's carrying amount, the asset is not impaired and there is no need to estimate the other amount.

## 11.4 Cash Generating Units

IAS 36 defines a cash generating unit (CGU) as the smallest identifiable group of assets that generates cash inflows that are largely independent of the cash inflows from other assets or groups of assets.

Where it is not possible to determine the recoverable amount for a single asset because it does not generate cash inflow, impairment test will be performed for the cash generating unit to which the asset belongs. A CGU can be a single asset. Assets like head office, goodwill, and other corporate/shared assets can be shared into cash generating units.

Impairment in a CGU should be accounted for by allocating the impairment to the assets within the CGU, firstly to goodwill and other assets on pro rata basis. It is the best practice to allocate impairment to any obsolete or damaged assets before applying the rules in IAS 36.

## 11.5 Recognition of impairment loss

The accounting entries required to record an impairment loss depend on whether the impaired asset had previously been revalued:

- **Asset held at Historical Cost:** Charge against profit or loss statement and credit non-current asset. The impaired loss charged to profit or loss statement is reported before operating profit, as an exceptional item if material.

- **Revalued Asset:** Charge against other comprehensive income (that is revaluation surplus) with the previous revalued amount and profit or loss statement with the excess impairment loss then credit non-current asset.

**Scenario 11.1: Impairment recognition**

iMax Ltd is proposing to stop the production of some of its expensive specialized products within the next two years as it is more profitable to import the finished goods from its parent than to produce the products locally. The useful life of assets used for the production of these products is five years, and the carrying value is N8million after the first year depreciation charge. Evaluate financial statements and tax effects.

There is a change in the useful life of the assets and should be accounted for prospectively in accordance with IAS 16. The reduction of useful life is an indication of impairment and management should recognize impairment loss of N4million in the current year. The net book value N4million would be depreciated over the two years accordingly.

The N6million charge against profit in the current year in respect of the asset would not be tax deductible. Capital allowance would be granted using the standard rate and deducted from assessable profit. This would give rise to a deductible temporary difference as the carrying value of the assets would be significantly less than the tax base. iMax would be required to carry out balancing adjustment when the assets become obsolete in two years.

## 11.6 When to test for impairment

An impairment test is required:
a. For all assets when there is an indication of impairment at the reporting date
b. Annually for certain assets:
- Goodwill acquired in a business combination
- Intangible assets with indefinite useful life
- Intangible assets which are not yet available for use

## 11.7  Reversal of Impairments:

The following are the general rules:
- An impairment loss on goodwill can never be reversed.
- An impairment loss on other assets or a CGU can be reversed where the recoverable amount has increased because of a change in economic conditions or expected use of the asset.
- The impairment loss can be reversed to the extent that the increased carrying amount of an individual asset does not exceed the amount that the asset would have been carried at had there been no initial impairment.
- A reversal of an impairment of a revalued asset is recognized as other comprehensive income and included in the revaluation surplus.

## 11.8  Indications of Impairment

Indications of impairment may be internal to a company or external. IAS 36 suggests the following indications should be considered:

**External Indicators**
- A decline in the asset's market value that is significantly greater than would be expected as a result of the passage of time or normal use. Changes in market values reflect economic conditions of the assets for example a change in demand for the asset's output.
- Significant adverse changes that have taken place or are expected in the near future in the technology, economic or legal environment or market the entity operates.
- Increase in interest rates or other market rates of return that may materially affect the discount rate used in calculating the asset's recoverable amount.
- The carrying amount of the entity's net assets exceeds the entity's market capitalization.

**Internal Indicators**
- Obsolescence or physical damage affecting the asset.
- Significant adverse changes that have taken place or are expected in the near future in the extent to which, or in the way that, an asset is used or expected to be used. This includes the asset becoming idle, plans to discontinue or restructure the operation to which the asset belongs or the asset's disposal. It also includes reassessing the assets useful life from indefinite to finite.
- Deterioration in the expected level of the asset's performance
- Management's own forecasts of future net cash inflows or operating profits may show a significant decline from previous budgets and forecasts

**Other Indicators**
- The actual net cash outflows or operating profit or loss may be significantly worse than budgeted
- Operating losses or net cash outflows are forecast
- Cash flows for constructing the asset or for maintaining or operating it are significantly higher than those budgeted.

### 11.9 Events after the reporting period

Events after the reporting period may provide indications that an asset was impaired at the year end. However, if the event indicates that the impairment occurred after the year end, the indicator is not taken into account, although disclosure in accordance with IAS 10 'Events after the balance sheet date' may be required.

The impairment test should be updated after the year end only if material changes in assumptions provide additional evidence relating to conditions that existed at the balance sheet date. This requires an analysis of facts and circumstances in order to distinguish between adjusting and non-adjusting information.

## 11.10 Tax Implications

**Corporation Tax**

An impairment loss is a charge against profit by reducing the cost or carrying value of an asset. The tax law does not permit any charge against profit apart from capital allowance for the use of assets.

Capital allowances are granted at standard rates for the use of qualifying capital expenditures. In computing adjusted/assessable profit, depreciation which represents an allowance for the wear and tear or passage of time for the use of assets charged against accounting profit is not tax deductible.

Impairment test is carried out on individual assets as well as cash generating units. This means, for the purpose of financial reporting, there could be more than one charges against profit in respect of a single asset; depreciation charge, impairment loss and impairment loss on the cash generating unit the asset belongs to.

Where the asset was previously revalued, impairment loss would be charged against revaluation surplus in other comprehensive income. The excess impairment loss over the valuation surplus on that asset would then be transferred into the profit or loss statement. In this instance, only the amount charged to profit or loss statement would be disallowed for income tax purpose.

Where there is a reversal of impairment, unless the asset has previously been revalued, the reversal will be recognized in the profit or loss statement and treated as non-taxable income for income tax purpose or recognized in other comprehensive income as revaluation surplus.

**Deferred Tax**

The carrying value of the asset will be reduced by the impairment loss in the statement of financial position. This could give rise to either deductible or taxable temporary difference. There is a deductible temporary difference where the carrying value of the asset is less than the tax base of the asset and the converse would be the case where there is a reversal of impairment thereby resulting to taxable temporary difference.

## References

IFRS RED Book 2012 PART A: 'the conceptual framework and requirements' and  PART B: 'the accompanying documents'
    IAS 36 Impairment of Assets
    IAS 10 Event after the reporting period
Companies Income Tax Act Cap C21 2004 LFN
Midaspage, Nigeria (2010) Tax Consequences of Adopting IFRS in Nigeria

# IAS 17: Lease Accounting

## 12.1 Introduction

IAS 17 defines a lease as an agreement whereby the lessor conveys to the lessee in return for a payment, or series of payments, the right to use an asset for an agreed period of time. This also covers contracts for the hire of an asset that give the hirer an option to acquire title to the asset (hire purchase contracts) and conditional sale agreements where title automatically passes to the lessee on making the final lease payment.

Leasing is a source of financing for companies such that, they gain the right to use an asset without paying for the full price as in an outright purchase transaction.

## 12.2  Classification of leases

IAS 17 classifies leases into finance and operating leases. Sale and leaseback transactions are also covered in this standard.

The basis for the classification is on the extent to which risks and rewards incidental to ownership of a lease asset lies with the lessor or with the lessee. The rewards derivable may be from the expectation of profitable operation over the asset's useful life and gains from the appreciation in value of the asset while the risk associated with assets include the possibilities of losses from idle capacity or technological obsolescence and of variation in earnings due to economic dwindling fortunes.

## 12.3 Finance Lease

A lease is classified as a finance lease if it transfers substantially all the risks and rewards incidental to ownership of an asset to the lessee. Below are other indicators where leases could be classified as finance leases:

- The lessor transfer ownership of the asset to the lessee by the end of the lease term.
- The lessee has the option to purchase the asset at a price that is expected to be sufficiently lower than the fair value at the date the option becomes exercisable.
- The lease term is for the majority of the useful life of the asset.
- At the beginning of the lease, the present value of the minimum lease payments is substantially equal to the fair value of the leased asset.
- The leased assets are so specialized that only the lessee can use them without major modification.
- The lessee bears the cost of cancelling the lease agreement.
- The lessee enjoys or bears any gain or loss arising from changes in fair value of the asset.
- The lessee has the opportunity to continue the lease for a secondary period at less than the market rent.

## 12.4 Operating Lease

This is any other lease other than a finance lease. Operating leases have the following features:

- Substantially all risks and rewards of ownership are not passed to the lessee.
- The lease is for a shorter period usually less than the useful economic life of the asset.
- The lessor recovers significant portion of his investment from the sale of the asset or a further hire after the end of the lease period.

## 12.5 Sale and Leaseback Transactions

This arises where an entity requiring funds sells a large asset, for example its head office building to a bank and immediately leases the building back on an annual rental basis and continues to occupy the building.

The issue for determination is whether, is it a true sale or it is obtaining a secured loan. Also, there is the need to ascertain whether the transaction is finance or an operating lease.

If it is a finance lease, the substance of the transaction is a secured loan. In this case, no sale is recorded and the proceeds or receipt from the sale is recorded as a loan and treated as follows:
- The excess of sales proceeds over the carrying amount in the books of the lessee or vendor should be deferred and amortized over the lease term.
- The risk and rewards of ownership remain with the lessee and the assets should be reported in the statement of financial position at its carrying value.
- Lease rental is to be separated as capital portion and interest element, reported in the statement of profit or loss and other comprehensive income.

If the leaseback is classified as an operating lease, the profit or loss arising on the sale is treated as follows:
- If the sales price is greater than the fair value of the asset; recognize the excess profit over the lease term.
- If the sales price is less than the fair value of the asset; recognize loss immediately unless a loss is compensated for by future below market lease payment, in which case, the loss is recognized over the lease term.
- If the fair value is equal to sale price but less than the carrying amount of the asset; recognize the loss immediately.

### Scenario 12.1: Lease Transaction

MSI Leasing leases 3 trucks to RoadNetworks for period of 4 years for N19.5million. The lease rentals are to be paid over six installments after an initial deposit of N4.5million. As at the date of the transaction, the market price of each truck stood at N6million with a residual value of N.3million after five years. RoadNetworks is to bear the insurance and the cost of maintenance of the trucks during the lease period. Evaluate financial statement and tax effects.

The lease should be classified as a finance lease, since the lease period covered substantial part of the economic useful life of the trucks and the lessee bears the risk of the assets. RoadNetworks should report N18million as the cost of non-current assets (the trucks) and finance liability of N1.5million in the statements of financial position. Depreciation and the portion of interest accrued should be charged to profit or loss statement annually.

The total interest charge of N1.5million is a revenue expenditure and tax deductible. The amount on which RoadNetworks would claim capital allowance is the capital portion of the deposit and the lease rental paid in the relevant years of assessments. RoadNetwork is required to withhold 10% tax at source from each lease rental payment. Finance lease are not taxable supplies therefore not liable to VAT.

## 12.6 Recognition and Measurement

Lease transactions are accounted for as follows:

### Finance lease

Assets acquired under finance lease are captured in the statement of the financial position of the lessee by debiting non-current asset and crediting a finance lease liability at the lower of fair value of the asset and the present value of the minimum lease payments.

The asset is depreciated over the shorter of the useful life of the asset and the lease term including any secondary lease term for below the market rentals. Depreciation charge is debited to profit or loss statement and credited to accumulated depreciation accordingly.

Interest is computed as the excess of the total payment to lessor over the fair value of the asset acquired (actuarial method). Accrued interest on outstanding liability is debited to finance cost to profit or loss statement and finance lease liability is credited accordingly. Finance lease liability is debited and bank is credited when lease rentals are paid. Lease rental payment has a capital and interest elements.

## Operating Lease

The lessee captures lease rental payments as expense in the profit or loss statement on a straight-line basis over the lease period. Any difference between the expense and amount paid is an accrual or prepayment in the statement of financial position.

### 12.7 Tax Implications

The following are the tax implications of lease transactions:
- The interest portion of the lease rental paid by the lessee is treated as an allowable expense for income tax purpose whether it is finance or operating lease.
- The lease rental received by the lessor is a taxable income for income tax purpose. Lease rentals under finance lease transaction are interest in nature therefore not VATable but treated as service charge for the use of assets under operating lease transactions and are VATable.
- The lessee is expected to withhold tax at source when making lease rentals payment. However this is usually impracticable in transactions where the lessor is a bank.
- Under a finance lease the lessee can claim capital allowance on the leased asset. The capital allowance to be claimed in any year of assessment is restricted to the capital portion of the lease rental paid.
- The Revenue will request for the lease contract agreement between the lessor and lessee to ascertain the true nature of transaction accordingly.

## References

IFRS RED Book 2012 PART A: 'the conceptual framework and requirements' and PART B: 'the accompanying documents'

    IAS 17 Leases

Companies Income Tax Act Cap C21 2004 LFN

FIRS Information Circular 2010/01 Guidelines on the Tax Implications of Leasing

Midaspage, Nigeria (2010) Tax Consequences of Adopting IFRS in Nigeria

# 13

## IAS 37: Provision and Contingencies

### 13.1 Introduction

IAS 37 defines the following key terms used in the standard:
- A provision is defined as a liability of uncertain timing or amount.
- A liability is defined as a present obligation of the entity arising from past events, the settlement of which is expected to result in an outflow from the entity of resources embodying economic benefits.

The word 'provision' is often used to describe amounts deducted from assets to arrive at their balance sheet carrying amount; for example, provisions for depreciation, provision for doubtful debts etc. Such provisions are not within the scope of IAS 37 because they relate to the measurement of assets and are merely adjustments made to arrive at the assets' appropriate carrying value.

IAS 37 does not permit provisions to be made for expenses and losses that are likely to arise in the future, for which there is no present obligation at the balance sheet date. It however covers:
- Undertaking major restructuring programmes.
- Accounting for decommissioning costs extractive and nuclear industries.
- Accounting for infrastructure asset maintenance programmes in water industry.
- Price controls in regulated industries.
- Environmental obligations

- Those that have outstanding litigations, particularly where off-setting insurance cover exists.
- Those that have onerous contacts.

## 13.2 Criteria for recognition

A provision is recorded in the financial statements where the following conditions are met:

- An entity has a **present obligation** (legal, contractual or constructive) as a result of past event.
- It is **probable** that an outflow of resources embodying economic benefits will be required to settle the obligation.
- A **reliable estimate** can be made of the amount of the obligation.

**a. Obligation:** This could be legal or constructive:

- A legal obligation is defined as an obligation derived from legal agreement or contract (explicit or implicit terms), legislation or other operations of law.
- A constructive obligation is defined as an obligation derived from an entity's actions where:
  i. By an established pattern of past practice, published policies or a sufficiently specific current statement, the entity has indicated to other parties that it will accept certain responsibilities; and
  ii. As a result, the entity has created a valid expectation on the part of those other parties that it will discharge those responsibilities.

**b. Probable:** IAS 37 states that an event is probable if the event is more likely than not to occur. Practically, this means that if an event has more than a 50% likelihood of occurring then it is probable.

**c. Reliable Estimate:** A reliable estimate of the amount of the obligation is a practical requirement in order that a provision can be made. IAS 37 states that a provision should be measured at:
  i. The best estimate of the expenditure required to settle the present obligation at the reporting date.

ii. Expected values where the provision involves a large population of items.

iii. Discounted to present value using a pre-tax rate where the time value of money is material. This is applicable where the settlement will be many years into the future.

## 13.3 Recognition and measurement

a. **Accounting for provisions:** A provision is created by charging the expense to the profit or loss statement and recognizing the provision in the statement of financial position. Subsequently, only the movement in the provision is recorded in the profit or loss statement.

However, there are certain cases where this accounting treatment differs:

- If a provision is discounted to its present value, and its settlement is some years in the future, it is initially recorded in the statement of position at its present value and as the provision increases by the years the discount is unwound. This unwinding of the discount is recorded as a finance charge in the profit or loss statement.

- If it involved the purchase of a non-current asset, there may be compulsory costs that are incurred at the end of the asset's life, for example, clean up or rectification costs to the site. These costs are provided for when the asset is initially purchased as the obligation exists at that point. They are recorded at present value if the time value of money is relevant, but the creation of the provision is not charged to the profit or loss statement. The accounting entry is to debit non-current asset, and credit provision. Essentially, the costs are capitalized into the initial cost of the asset. The only charge to the profit or loss statement is the unwinding of the discount on the provision each year.

## Scenario13.1: Accounting for provision

Elite Oil and Gas Co, is an exploration and production company in the Nigerian oil and gas industry. The company has spilled oil causing damage that will cost N16 million to clean. There is no environmental legislation but the company has clear green policies on its websites. The company has also constructed an oil rig at the cost of N200 million and will cost N100 million to install. The license obtained from Federal Government had an agreement to dismantle the rig at the end of 20 years. The cost of dismantling the rig is estimated at N120 million and the appropriate discount rate is 10%. Evaluate financial statement and tax effects.

IAS 37 states the criteria for making provisions in the financial statements. In this case, there is a constructive obligation which has created a valid expectation that the company will clean up the environment given the public green policy on its websites. The cost has been reliably estimated at N16million and highly probable that the company will incur the cost. At the end of the reporting date, Elite Oil and Gas should charge N16 million as exceptional cost in the profit or loss statement and report a provision in the statement of financial position for the same amount.

The charge to profit or loss statement would not be tax deductible until the expense has been incurred and paid. This will create a deferred tax asset and the carrying amount would be less than the tax base at the reporting date.

There is a legal obligation to dismantle the oil rig; the amount has been reliably estimated as N120 million and it is highly probable that the company will incur the expense when the rig is dismantled.

The initial cost of asset will be N318 million (N200m + 100 + 18) in the statement of financial position being cost of construction, installation and dismantling. The N18million (N120m/$1.1^{20}$) is arrived at as a provision for the N120 million liability, being the discounted present value of the future cash outflow.

Annually, depreciation of N15.9milliom (N318m/20) and a finance charge of N1.8million (10% of N18million) should be charged to the profit or loss statement and credited to the statement of financial position accordingly.

Elite Oil and Gas will be entitled to capital allowance claim on the N318million and the finance charge allowed as revenue expenditure for income tax purpose.

**b. Accounting for contingencies:** This is classified as contingent liabilities and assets:

**A contingent liability** is defined as a possible obligation that arises from past events and whose existence will be confirmed only by the occurrence or non-occurrence of one or more uncertain future events not within the control of the entity; or a present obligation that arises from past events but is not recognized because:
   i. It is not probable that an outflow of resources embodying economic benefits will be required to settle the obligation or
   ii. The amount of the obligation cannot be measured with sufficient reliability.
- A contingent liability should not be recognized in the statement of financial position.
- If a transfer of economic benefits is possible, the contingency should be disclosed in the notes to the financial statements
- If a transfer of economic benefits is remote, the contingency is ignored for the purposes of the preparation of the financial statements.

**A contingent asset** is defined as a possible asset that arises from past events and whose existence will be confirmed only by the occurrence or non-occurrence of one or more uncertain future events not wholly within the control of the entity.
- If the likelihood of economic inflows is considered either possible or remote, a contingent asset is ignored for the purpose of the

preparation of the financial statements.
- If the likelihood of economic inflows is considered probable, a contingent asset is disclosed in the notes to the financial statements.
- If economic inflows are virtually certain, the asset is no longer contingent and should be recognized.

### 13.4 Tax Implications

For the purpose of tax, specific provisions are allowed while general provisions are not tax deductible expense. Within the scope of IAS 37, provisions are obligations that are probable with reliable estimates: The following treatments will apply:

**a. Provisions not involving the purchase of assets**
This could be constructive or legal obligations that are probable and the amount can be reliably estimated. For example, provisions made towards environmental cleaning, a proposed organization restructuring will involve creating an expense in the profit or loss statement and a liability in the statement of financial position.

The charge to profit or loss statement will not be tax deductible expense until it is funded. That is, there is economic outflow from the entity or the expense representing the provision is paid for by the reporting entity.

This will give rise to a deferred tax asset since the carrying amount of the liability is greater than its tax base. This is expected to reverse when the provision is funded and the expense becomes tax deductible.

**b. Provisions involving the purchase of assets**
A good example of decommissioning cost of an asset is an oil rig. The initial provision added to the cost of the asset should be entitled to capital allowance claim while the depreciation will be disallowed for income tax purposes.

The subsequent unwind amount or finance cost charged to the profit or loss statement should be treated as revenue expenditure and allowed for tax purpose. This will also have impact on the deferred tax computation of the reporting entity.

### c. Contingent Assets and Liabilities

Until it is probable that economic inflow/outflow of resources to or from the entity and reported in the financial statements, contingent assets and liabilities are remote and are left out of the financial statements or disclosed as notes to financial statements only. The tax implications are very remote.

### References

IFRS RED Book 2012 PART A: 'the conceptual framework and requirements' and PART B: 'the accompanying documents'

IAS 37 Provisions, Contingent Liabilities and Contingent Assets

Companies Income Tax Act Cap C21 2004 LFN

Midaspage, Nigeria (2010) Tax Consequences of Adopting IFRS in Nigeria

# IAS 2: Inventories

## 14.1 Introduction

IAS 2 Inventories prescribe the accounting treatment for inventories, the amount of cost to be recognized as an asset and carried forward until the related revenues are recognized. Inventories are assets:
- Held for sale in the ordinary course of business
- In the process of production for such sale; or
- In the form of materials or supplies to be consumed in the production process or in the rendering of services.

Net realizable value is the estimated selling price in the ordinary course of business less the estimated cost of completion and the estimated cost necessary to make the sale.

IAS 2 Inventories applies to all inventories such as raw materials, consumable supplies, work in progress and finished goods. The following are not covered within the scope of the standard:
- Work in progress arising from under construction contracts, including directly related service contracts covered by IAS 11 Construction Contracts.
- Financial Instruments covered by IAS 39 Financial Instruments
- Biological assets related to agricultural activity and agricultural produce at the point of harvest covered by IAS 41 Agriculture.

## 14.2 Recognition of inventories

An entity shall recognize an asset as inventory if it meets the definition of inventory and has control of the inventory for which future economic benefits will flow to the entity, and the cost of the inventory can be reliably measured. The following assets are to be recognized as inventory:

- Property acquired for resale under the course of the ordinary activities of the entity.
- Investment property transfer to inventories with a view to sale.
- Property constructed for the specific purpose of resale if the business model of the entity is to sell such properties.

### 14.3 Measurement of inventories

Inventories are initially measured at cost and subsequently measured at the lower of cost and net realizable value. Principal situations in which net realizable value may be lower than cost include:

- An increase in cost or a fall in selling price
- Physical deterioration in the condition of inventory
- Obsolescence of products
- Company's marketing strategy to lower prices
- Errors in production or purchasing

The cost of inventories shall comprise all cost of purchase, cost of conversion and other costs incurred in bringing the inventories to their present location and condition. The three components of inventories are:

- **Cost of purchase**: This comprises the purchase price, import duties and other taxes (other than those subsequently recoverable by the entity from the taxing authority), transport, handling and other cost directly attributable to the acquisition of finished goods, materials and services less trade discounts, rebates etc.

- **Cost of Conversion**: This comprises cost directly related to the units of production such as direct materials and direct labours, and a systematic allocation of fixed and variable production overheads that are incurred in converting materials into finished goods.

- **Other Cost**: incurred in bring the inventories to their present condition and location.

The following costs are to be excluded from the cost of inventory and recognized as expenses in the period in which they are incurred:
- Abnormal amounts of wasted materials, labour or other production costs
- Storage cost after the production stage.
- Administrative overheads
- Selling costs

### 14.4 Recognition of an Expense

The costs of inventories are to be charged to Profit or Loss Statement where:
- Inventories are sold; the carrying amount is recognized as expense in the period in which the related revenue is recognized.
- There is write-down of inventories to net realizable value; the amount is recognized as expense in the period the write-down or loss occurs.
- There is a write-back as a result of increase in net realizable value; the amount written back shall be recognized as a reduction to the cost of inventories to be recognized as expense for the period the reversal occurs.
- An entity purchases inventories on deferred settlement terms; the financing element is recognized as interest expense over the period of the financing.
- Inventories are used as a component of self-constructed property, plant and equipment; the inventories are to be recognized as an expense during the useful life of the assets.

### 14.5 Inventory Cost Formulas

IAS 2 prohibits the use of Last in, First-out (LIFO). The two techniques recommended are First-in, First-out (FIFO) and Weighted average cost methods.

Inventories that are ordinarily interchangeable shall be valued using either first-in, first out or the weight average cost formulas. The same cost formulas must be applied to all inventories having a similar nature and use to the entity while inventories with a different nature or use, different cost formulas may be justified.

Inventory segregated for specific projects or contracts; the cost attributable to the items of inventory should be individually identified.

### 14.6 Tax implications

#### Income Tax
The cost of inventory relating to sales in any financial year are subsumed in the cost of sale or direct costs and allowed for income tax purpose. Write-down to net realizable value charged to profit or loss statement on item by item basis should be allowed for income tax.

While a general write-off of inventory will not be allowed, where inventories are stolen or destroyed, the cost of such inventories should be allowed except if the entity has insured the inventories.

#### Value Added Tax
The purchase cost inventory may include VAT and other taxes. Where the VAT is offset-able from the Output VAT therefore the input VAT should not constitute the cost of purchase. Where the input VAT is not offset-able because the entity's products are VAT exempted or Zero rated, input VAT will be part of purchase cost of the inventories if the products are VAT exempted. The input VAT will not be part of the cost of inventories if the entity's products are zero-rated, however, the entity would claim VAT refund.

#### Reclassification of Assets
The transition to IFRS will give rise to reclassification of some assets from current assets to non-current assets and vice versa. Examples will include returnable containers, inventories use as components

of property, plant and equipment. VAT on non-current assets are capitalized and capital allowance is claimed on the total amount while VAT on current assets are subjected to the Input and Output VAT process.

At transition, the treatment of capital allowance and VAT should be maintained until the existing assets are fully written off or consumed.

## References

IFRS RED Book 2012 PART A: 'the conceptual framework and requirements' and PART B: 'the accompanying documents'
    IAS 2 Inventories
Companies Income Tax Act Cap C21 2004 LFN
Midaspage, Tax & IFRS Academy (2012) IFRS: Tax Implications

# 15

## IAS 19: Employee Benefits

### 15.1 Introduction

IAS 19 is the accounting standard that deals with employees' short term and long term benefits, except share options used to reward employees for services as covered in IFRS 2 Share-based Payment.

The standard requires that an employer should report a liability in the financial statements when an employee provides service in exchange for benefits to be paid in the future. This approach is in consonance with asset and liability recognition proposition of the IASB framework for financial reporting.

The scope of IAS 19 covers employee benefits payable during employment and post-employment benefits.

### 15.2 Employee benefits payable during employment

Benefits payable during employment can be classified as follows:

**a. Short-term benefits:** These include salaries, wages, bonuses, leave allowance benefits-in-kind, etc, payable within twelve months of the year end of a reporting entity.

**b. Long-term benefits:** These include long-term incentive plans, long-service award, redundancy pay and other bonuses payable, twelve months after the reporting entity's year end.

## 15.3 Employee benefits payable after employment

IAS 19 defines post-employment benefits as employee benefits (other than termination benefits) which are payable after the completion of employment. Examples include pensions, post-retirement medical or health care, post-retirement life insurance etc.

Employers meet their obligations of post-employment benefits through various types of benefit plans such as:

**a. Defined contribution plans:** Are post-employment benefit plans under which an entity pays fixed contribution into a separate entity (a fund) and will have no legal or constructive obligation to pay further contributions if the fund does not hold sufficient assets to pay all employee benefits relating to employee service in the current and prior periods.

Defined contribution plans are pension also referred to as money purchase plans where the benefit to employee depend on the value of contribution made and the performance of the investment.

**b. Defined benefit plans:** Are post-employment benefit plans other than defined contribution plans. Defined benefit plans are pension which specify the benefit to be paid usually based on a percentage of the employee's final salary or average pay over a defined period and financed accordingly.

In this type of benefit plan, the employer bears the risk of any poor performance of the investment; consequently the employer's liability is not limited.

## 15.4 Recognition and Measurement

The following accounting treatments are applicable to employee benefits below:

**a. Short-term benefits:** An expense is recognized in the profit or loss statement when the employee has rendered services in exchange for the benefit and a liability where payments are outstanding. An example is when an entity has legal or constructive obligation to make payments as a result of past events in form of profit sharing or performance bonuses etc.

Capitalization of employees' benefits may also be required in line with other standards.

**b. Post-employment benefits**: A liability is recognized in the statement of financial position when employees have provided services in exchange for benefits to be paid in future.

Plan assets (long-term employee benefit funds or investments) are measured at fair value at each reporting date. Actuarial valuation methods are used to measure the plan liability (defined benefit obligation) by discounting to present value. The difference would give rise to a surplus or a deficit. A surplus is regarded as asset and a deficit is regarded as a liability.

The pension liability to be reported in the statement of financial position is the excess of the obligation over the fund while expense is recognized in the profit or loss statement which may not necessarily reflect the contributions made in the period.

In a funded plan, plan assets are held in an entity (fund) that is legally separate from the entity. In the case of unfunded plan, the entity recognizes the gross amount of the plan liability and makes plans to pay the retirement benefits itself.

c. **Long-term benefits:** These are accounted for in the same way as defined benefit pension. However, all past service costs are recognized immediately on the profit or loss while actuarial gains and losses are recognized immediately through other comprehensive income.

d. **Termination benefits:** A liability should be recognized when an entity has a demonstrable commitment, which may be legal, contractual or constructive either to; provide terminal benefits to encourage voluntary redundancy or terminate the employment of a staff or group of staff before normal retirement date. The provision should be made in line with the principles of IAS 37, Provisions, contingent liabilities and contingent assets.

### 15.5 Tax Implications

Taxation of income accruing to individuals in employment is covered under the Personal Income Tax Act Cap P8 2004 LFN as amended. Employees are assessed to tax either through Direct Assessment or through the Pay-As-You-Earn (PAYE) scheme. The Act however distinguishes between taxable benefits and non-taxable benefits:

### a. Taxable benefits

These include both short-term and long-term benefits paid to employees during employments. Short-term benefits such as salaries and wages, allowances and bonuses, benefits-in-kind or perquisites are assessed to tax on actual year basis through the PAYE scheme.

Short-term benefits such as housing allowance, transport allowance, utility allowance, entertainment allowance, lunch allowance and leave allowance are now liable to tax.

Long-term benefits such as long service award, profit sharing or performance bonuses, and redundancy pay are assessed to tax when paid. The tax liability payable can be arrived at by applying the effective rate of tax of each employee on the amount paid to them.

### b. Non-taxable benefits

This covers only short-term benefits to employees during employment such as provision of meal in staff canteen, provision of uniform, overall or other protective clothing, and any sum received for expenses incurred by an employee in the performance of his duties for which it is not intended that the employee will make any profit or gain.

## c. Loans to employees

Where employers grants interest free loan or below the market-rate loans to employee, the employees shall be deemed to have earned a taxable benefit equal to the difference between the present value of the future expected cash flows and the loan amount granted to the employee.

## d. Post Employment Benefits

This includes benefits paid after employment such as pension, gratuity, terminal pay and termination of employment pay or compensation for loss of office.

Terminal pay is taxable. Gratuity pay, lump-sum received from pension provident fund and compensation for loss of office are tax exempt. Also, monthly pension received are exempted from Personal Income Tax in consonance with the Pension Reforms Act 2004.

## d. Corporation Tax

Employee benefits, short-term or long-term are reported as staff cost in the profit or loss statements. The staff cost is made up of the payroll cost and other employees' benefits.

For income tax computations, all payroll costs are tax deductible while other employee benefits such as provision for gratuity, pension, redundancy etc are not tax deductible until when actual payment is made. This will impact on the deferred tax account of the reporting entity.

With respect to interest free loan or below the market-rate loan to employee, the fair value of the benefits (interest chargeable) will be adjusted for and taxed accordingly. The tax authority will argue that the interest chargeable is the opportunity cost forgone to the entity.

Also, the amount that is allowed for income tax as cost to company for any benefit or allowance provided for senior staff and executives of any entity shall be restricted to the amount prescribed by the collective agreement between the entity and the employees and approved by the Federal Ministry responsible for labour matters.

## References

IFRS RED Book 2012 PART A: 'the conceptual framework and requirements' and PART B: 'the accompanying documents'

    IAS 19 Employee Benefits

    IFRIC 14 The Limit on a Defined Benefit Asset, Minimum Funding Requirements and their Interaction

Personal Income Tax Act Cap P8 2004 LFN

Companies Income Tax Act Cap C21 2004 LFN

Midaspage, Nigeria (2010) Tax Consequences of Adopting IFRS in Nigeria

# 16

# IFRS 2: Share-Based Payment

## 16.1 Introduction

IFRS 2 defines a share-based payment as a transaction where an entity receives or acquires goods or services either as consideration for its equity instruments or by incurring liabilities for amounts based on the price of the entity's shares or other equity instruments of the entity.

The objective of IFRS 2 is to specify the accounting requirements for an entity when it undertakes a share-based payment transaction. In particular, it requires an entity to reflect in its profit or loss statement and statement of financial position, the effects of share-based payment transactions, including expenses associated with transactions in which share options are granted to employees.

- Grant date is the date an entity and another party agree to a share-based payment transaction.

- Vesting period is the time period that the conditions of the share-based payment transaction are satisfied.

- Vesting conditions are the terms and conditions required to be fulfilled. For example, employees may be granted share options which will be vested after a certain number of years of service. Alternatively, there may be performance target set, such that the employee receives shares only when the targets are met.

## 16.2 The scope of IFRS 2

IFRS 2 applies to any transaction where an entity receives goods or services in exchange for a transfer of its own equity instruments of an existing shareholder or itself or of its parent or another member of the group which will involve:

- The use of share options plan for the purpose of employee remuneration either as a management incentive or through employee share purchase plans that are available to all employees.
- Share-based payment used as a method by which entities procure other goods or services.

There are three types of share-based payment transactions:
- **Equity-settled share-based payments transaction:** Where the transaction involves the receipt of goods or services settled with an entity's own equity instruments such as:

a. Employee share option plan
  b. Employee share plan, including employee share purchase plans and share incentive plans
  c. Transactions in which an entity obtains goods or services in exchange for its own equity instruments. For example, start-up companies may obtain consultancy and similar services in exchange for shares, thus preserving scarce cash resources and giving the supplier an opportunity to share in the company's success.

**Cash-settled share-based payment transaction:** Where an entity acquires goods or services and agrees to pay cash for the goods or services based on the entity's share price at the date of settlement.

**Transactions that could be settled either by equity or cash:** The choice of the mode of settlement depends on either the entity or the supplier.

## 16.3 Recognition of Share-Based Payment Transactions

The goods or services acquired in a share-based payment transaction should be recognized, either as an expense or as an increase in assets, when they are received.

If an entity grants share option to its employees provided that they remain in the employment of the entity say for a period of three years, the cost is recognized in the profit or loss statement over the period and corresponding accounting entry is an increase in equity.

For a cash-settled share-based payment transaction, a liability is recognized and re-measured at each reporting date.

## 16.4 Measurement of Share-Based Payment Transactions

IFRS 2 requires an entity to measure the goods or services received and the corresponding increase in equity at fair value. Fair value is defined as 'the amount for which an asset could be exchanged, a liability settled, or an equity instrument granted could be exchanged, between knowledgeable, willing parties in an arm's length transaction'.

**Equity Settled Transactions:** Cost is recognized as the fair value of the goods and services received. If the goods and services cannot be measured reliably, then the cost recognized is the fair value of the equity instruments granted at the grant date. The cost is recognized over the vesting period.

If an entity grants share options to employees, the cost to be recognized is the fair value of the share options at the grant date. This is due to the difficulty of measuring the cost of employee services received.

**Cash-Settled Transactions:** Cash settled transaction include share appreciation rights where a third party is entitled to a cash payment which is dependent on the entity's share price. For example, if the share price rises over the specified period of time before payment, then the amount of cash paid will increase. In this case the entity measures the liability at fair value. This liability is re-measured at the year end until settlement.

## 16.5 Accounting for Share-Based Payment Transactions

a. **Equity-Settled:** Are recognized at fair value at the grant date. The cost is then allocated over the vesting period. The formula for calculating the equity at the year end is:

| Number of rights vesting period | X | Fair value at grant date | X | Fraction of vesting period |
|---|---|---|---|---|

The amount to be charged to the profit or loss statement is the difference between the current year-end balance and the previous year-end balance.

### Scenario 16.1: Equity-settled transactions

Amadi Trading Ltd has its accounting year end as 31st December. In the year ended 31st December 2010, the company carried out the following transaction.

On March 2, issued fully paid shares to 5 directors and the shares issued to the directors normally have vesting condition that they remain in the company's employment for the next three years. However, the directors were issued the shares because of their performance in the immediate past year. The market value of the shares issued was N100 million as at that date. Evaluate financial statement and tax effect.

Generally, the fair value of the goods or services obtained by the entity is used to measure the consideration payable for employee services or goods acquired. The transaction is an equity-settled share-based payment. However, since the share options are based on services rendered and no other enforceable vesting conditions, profit or loss statement will be charged with N100milion while the same amount would be credited to share capital in the statement of financial position at year end.

The charge to profit or loss statement under operating cost (staff cost) will be tax deductible for corporate tax purpose. The directors would be deemed to have earned a taxable benefit liable to personal income tax using the effective tax rate applicable to each director on the income that has accrued to them. Gains arising from disposal of the shares will be exempted from Capital Gain Tax. However any dividend received on the shares would suffer tax deduction at source at the rate of 10% as the final tax.

**b. Cash-Settled**: A liability is recognized in the statement of financial position and this will change each year end depending on the share price or fair value of share options. As the cash paid is linked to the price of the shares, the liability is re-measured at the year-end using the share price or fair value of options in the calculation.

**Scenario 16.2: Cash-settled share-based payment**
The facts are the same as in case 16.1. On 15th May, the company granted share appreciation rights to pay for the purchase of inventory worth N6million and at the reporting date, the value of the shares were N6.7million. Evaluate the financial Statements and tax effects.

This is a cash-settled share-based payment transaction. Amadi Trading incurs a liability which will be settled based on its share price. To recognize the fair value of the liability incurred is to debit inventory by N6.7million and credit trade creditors with same amount in the statement of financial position at the reporting date.

The inventory is an asset which will generate economic benefit or revenue liable to corporate tax, and VAT if the goods are taxable supplies. The cost of the inventory will be tax deductible captured as cost of sales in the profit or loss statements.

## 16.6 Tax Implications

Share-based payment transactions would give rise to the following tax issues:

**Corporation tax**

The consideration received either in cash or equity by the contracting entity for sale of goods or services will constitute revenue liable to corporation tax. Also, the cost of acquiring goods or services should be reported as part of operating expenses or cost of sales and would be regarded as allowable expenses incurred in the ordinary course of carrying out the entity's business for tax purposes.

However, the amount allowable for income tax purpose shall be the intrinsic value of the share options which is the difference between the market price of the options and the exercise price of the options.

For transactions involving services rendered by employees, the cost recognized in the financial statements would not be allowed for income tax since the transaction does not involve cash payment. When the options are exercised, the amount allowable for tax deduction shall be the intrinsic value of share options which is the difference between the market price of the options and the exercise price of the options.

This will give rise to deductible temporary difference as the expense in the profit or loss statement is not deductible until future periods.

**Employee Taxes**

As the share options vested, the entity would recognize a cost on its profit or loss statement; staff cost under operating expenses and the employees would be deemed to have earned income liable to PAYE tax. However, under a share appreciation right arrangement the taxable benefit that will be deemed to have accrued; would be the difference in the amount paid by the employees on the shares between the option date and when the share right was exercised.

## Deferred Tax on SBP

IFRS 2 specifies how to recognize deferred tax in the financial statements on transactions involving share-based payment. Deferred tax on SBP will arise where the contract is spanning more than one year and a portion of the expense will not be recognized in the profit or loss statement until future periods.

Deferred tax on Share-Based Payment is determined as follows:

DT Asset = $\dfrac{\text{No of right expected to vest}}{}$ x Intrinsic value x Timing ratio x Tax rate

## References

IFRS RED Book 2012 PART A: 'the conceptual framework and requirements' and PART B: 'the accompanying documents'

IFRS 2 Share-based Payment

Companies Income Tax Act Cap C21 2004 LFN

Personal Income Tax Act Cap P8 2004 LFN as amended

Midaspage, Nigeria (2010) Tax Consequences of Adopting IFRS in Nigeria

# IAS 32, 39 & IFRS 7: Financial Instruments

## 17.1 Introduction

Financial Instruments are contracts that give rise to a financial asset of one entity and a financial liability or equity instrument of another entity.

| Financial Assets | Financial Liabilities | Equities |
|---|---|---|
| • Cash | • Payables | • Ordinary Shares issued |
| • Ordinary Shares held in another company | • Redeemable loan stock | • Irredeemable preference shares issued |
| • Loan Stock held in another company | • Convertible loan stock issued | • Loan Stock held in another company |
| • Receivables | • Redeemable preference shares issued | • Receivables |

Figure 17.1: Financial Instruments Classification

## 17.2 Classifications

### a. Financial asset at fair value through profit or loss (FVTPL):
A financial asset is classified as fair value through profit or loss where it is acquired principally for resale (held for trading) e.g.
- Ordinary shares in another company held for short term
- Loan stock in another company held for short term

**Held to maturity (HTM):** A financial asset is classified as held to maturity where an entity intends to hold the asset to maturity and the asset has fixed or determinable maturity date and payments e.g.

- A fixed interest loan stock in another company intended to be held until redemption

**c. Loans and receivables:** A financial asset is classified as loan and receivable if it:
- Has fixed or determinable payments
- Is not quoted in an active market
- Is not held for trading or intention to sell in the short term
- Is not designated as available-for-sale

Examples are bank loans and trade receivables

**d. Available-for-sale (AFS)**: Example of available-for-sale financial asset is holding ordinary shares in another company for long term. AFS are assets not classified as FVTPL, HTM and loans and receivables.

**e. Financial Liabilities at fair value through profit or loss (FVTPL)**: Financial liabilities held for trading or acquired principally for resale. Examples are derivatives.

**f. Financial Liabilities**: Other financial liabilities measured at amortized cost, examples include trade payables and bank loans.

### 17.3 Recognition and Measurement

**a. Initial Recognition:** Financial Instruments are recognized in an entity's statement of financial position at fair value. In case of financial asset, it is the fair value plus the transaction cost while financial liabilities are recognized based on the proceeds received after deducting the transaction cost.

**b. Subsequent measurement:** This will depend on the class of the financial instrument as follows:

| Classes | Statement of Financial Position | Profit or Loss Statement | Other Comprehensive Income |
|---------|--------------------------------|--------------------------|----------------------------|
| Financial Asset FVTPL | Re-measured at fair value at each reporting date | Gains and losses recognized as part of profit<br><br>Interest and dividend as part of profit | |
| Financial Asset Held to Maturity | Measured at amortized cost | Interest recognized as finance income | |
| Financial Assets Loans & receivables | Measured at amortized cost | Interest recognized as finance income | |
| Financial Asset Available for Sale | Re-measured at fair value at each reporting date | Interest and dividend recognized as part of profit | Gains and losses recognized and credited or charged to reserves |
| Financial Liabilities FVTPL | Re-measured at fair value at each reporting date | Gains and losses recognized as part of profit<br><br>Interest and dividend as part of profit | |
| Financial Liabilities | Measured at amortized cost | Interest recognized as finance cost | |

Figure 17.2 Financial Instrument Recognition and Measurement

**c. Fair Value:** Fair Value is defined as the price that will be received to sell an asset or pay to transfer a liability in an orderly transaction between market participants at the measurement date. It suffices to posit that a financial instrument's initial fair value will normally be the transaction price, that is, the fair value of the consideration given or received.

**d. Amortized Cost:** This is defined as the amount of initial recognition minus principal repayment, plus or minus the cumulative amortization of any difference between that initial amount and the amount payable at maturity and minus any reduction for impairment. For example, a redeemable debt issued is measured at the proceeds received less issue cost. This may be issued at a discount or redeemed at a premium.

**Scenario 17.1: Accounting for financial instrument**

Evaluate the financial statement and tax effects of the following investments made by HTCables during the financial year ended 31st December 2009:

Bought N13million investment classified as available-for-sale on 1st June. The fair value as at year end was N14million. Transaction cost on the investment was N500, 000.00

On 3rd October, purchased N700, 000.00 investment incurring transaction cost of N30, 000.00. The intention is to hold the investment at most for six months. The fair value of the investment at year end was N675, 000.00.

For Available-for-sale financial asset, HTCables would recognize N13.5million, being the acquisition and transaction cost on the transaction date in the statement of financial position. At year end, AFS financial asset would be carried at a fair value of N14million and the fair value gain of N500, 000.00 reported in other comprehensive income. Fair value gains on AFS financial assets are regarded as capital gain and therefore not liable to income tax. Also, gains on stocks and securities are exempted from capital gains tax.

Fair value through profit and loss financial assets is generally investment held for short-term trading or speculation. On the transaction date, cost of N730,    000.00 should be recognized as financial asset on the statement of financial position. At year end, the carrying value should be reported as N675, 000.00 and loss on financial asset of N55, 000.00 should be charged to the profit or loss statement. The loss on financial asset is not tax deductible since the gain on financial assets is currently exempted from income tax and capital gains tax.

It is important to posit that the intention in the distinction between financial assets classified as Available- for- Sale (AFS) and Fair Value through Profit or Loss (FVTPL) should provide a pointer to settling the long age debate on the tax status of gains from stock and securities. It is clear that AFS financial assets are investment held for long-term which should not be liable to income tax and capital gain while FVTPL financial assets are investment held for trading and should be liable to income tax accordingly.

Effective January 2012, gains or profit on security instruments are now exempted from income tax.

### 17.4 Impairment of financial Assets:

Financial assets measured at amortized cost such as held to maturity and loans and receivable would be deemed to be impaired when their carrying value exceeds the present value of the future cash flows discounted at the financial asset's original effective interest rate. Also, available-for-sale financial assets are impaired when the changes in their fair values are recognized in other comprehensive income.

Financial assets carried at fair value through profit or loss, are not tested for impairment. Any diminution in value of the financial asset is impairment already reflected in the fair value.

IAS 39 deals with impairment of financial assets as follows:

- To determine whether there is objective evidence that a financial asset or group of financial assets are impaired at each reporting date.
- If there is objective evidence of impairment, the entity should measure and recognize the impairment loss at the reporting date
- The measurement of impairment losses differs between financial assets carried at amortized cost, financial assets carried at cost and available-for-sale financial assets.

**Scenario 17.2: Impairment for financial instruments**

Wyse Finance Ltd offered N200, 000.00 loan facility to JFBiodun & Co on 1st of March 2005. The loan is repayable by 28th February 2009. JFBiodun is to pay interest at the end of each year. The effective interest rate is 8%. The directors of Wyse Finance Ltd got the news that JFBiodun is in financial difficulties and currently undergoing a financial reorganization. Though the interest for the year ended 28th February 2007 has just been paid, Wyse Finance Ltd directors perceived that they will only receive N100,000.00 by 28th February 2009 and no further interest payment is likely to be received. Evaluate financial statement and tax effects as at the year ended 28th February 2007.

IAS 39 requires an entity to assess at each reporting date whether there is objective evidence that its financial assets are impaired. In this case, the financial difficulties and reorganization of JFBiodun constitute objective evidence that the loan is impaired.

An impairment loss of N114, 267.00 (N200, 000-N85, 733) should be recognized in the profit or loss statement as at 28th February 2007. The impairment loss is arrived at by discounting the estimated future cash flow N100, 000.00 receivable on 28th February 2009 to the present value using the effective interest rate of 8%.

The impairment loss would be regarded as specific provision on loan loss allowed as deductible expense for tax purposes. The impairment will impact on the deferred tax balance of the financial asset accordingly.

**17.5 Financial assets carried at amortized cost:**

Examples are loans and receivables or held-to maturity financial assets. If there is objective evidence that an impairment loss on such an asset has been incurred, the amount of the loss should be measured as the difference between the asset's carrying amount and the present value of estimated future cash flows, discounted at the financial asset's original effective interest rate (the effective interest rate computed at initial recognition). The expected cash flows should exclude future credit losses that have not been incurred.

The standard allows the carrying amount of the asset to be reduced either by direct write-down or through the use of an allowance account such as a loan loss provision or provision for bad and doubtful debts. However, the amount of the loss should be recognized on the income statement.

### a. Evaluation of impairment on a portfolio basis

The assessment process for measuring impairment losses of a group of financial assets carried at amortized cost is as follows:

- First, financial assets that are considered to be individually significant are assessed for impairment individually if there is objective evidence of impairment.
- Secondly, all other assets that are not individually significant are assessed for impairment. They may be assessed either individually or collectively on a group basis as indicated below.
- Thirdly, all assets that have been individually assessed for impairment, whether significant or not, but for which there is no objective evidence of impairment, are included within a group of assets with similar credit risk characteristics and collectively assessed for impairment.
- Fourthly, assets that are individually assessed for impairment and for which an impairment loss is (or continue to be) recognized are not included in a collective assessment for impairment.

### b. General impairment for bad and doubtful debts

As it is common for entities under some local accounting standard to determine bad debt impairments for non-performing loans based on a matrix or similar formula that specifies fixed impairment rates for the number of days a loan or a debt is overdue.

For example, the impairment rates provided by the CBN prudential guideline on loan loss provisioning by bank specifies facilities:

- Outstanding for more than 90 days but less than 180 days provision of 10%
- Outstanding for more than 180 days but less than 365 day provision of 50%
- Outstanding for more than 365 days, 100% provision

Such a method of impairment is not acceptable under IAS 39, unless it produces a result that is sufficiently close to the one obtained by following the discounted cash flow methodology which is considered highly unlikely.

## 17.6 The CBN Prudential Guideline – Loan loss provisioning

Credit facilities (which include loans, advances, overdrafts, commercial paper, bankers' acceptance, bill discounted, leases, guarantees, and other loss contingencies connected with a bank's credit risk) should be classified as either performing or non-performing as defined below:

- A credit facility is deemed to be performing if payments of both principal and interest are up-to-date in accordance with the agreed terms.
- A credit facility should be deemed as non-performing when the interest or principal is due and unpaid for 90 days or more or interest payment equal to 90 days interest or more have been capitalized, rescheduled or rolled over into a new loan.

The guideline states that in order for banks to reflect their true financial condition, two provisions, that is, general and specific are required:

**a. General provision:** This is to be made in recognition that even performing credit facility harbours some risk of loss no matter how small.

**b. Specific provision:** This is further classified as non-specialized loans and specialized loans

**i. Non-specialized loans:** For principal repayments not yet due on non-performing credit facilities, provision should be made as follows:
- Sub-standard credit facilities: 10% of the outstanding balance
- Doubtful credit facilities: 50% of the outstanding balance
- Lost credit facilities: 100% of the outstanding balance

**ii. Specialized loans:** The classification and provisioning for specialized loans such as Agricultural finance, Project finance, Real Estate finance, SME finance and Mortgage finance takes into considerations the cash flows and gestation periods of the different loan types. For example, the provision on non-performing agric loan classified as long-term facility is as follows:

- Watch-list overdue by 90 days: 0% of the outstanding balance
- Sub-standard overdue by 90 days to 1 year: 25% of outstanding balance
- Doubtful overdue by 1 to 2 years: 50% of outstanding balance
- Very doubtful overdue by 2 to 3 years: 75% of outstanding balance
- Loss overdue by more than 3 years: 100% of outstanding balance

### 17.7 Alignment of Prudential Guideline to IFRS

The CBN has stated that the provisions under the prudential guideline should be aligned to the provisions under IFRS and to recognize the impact in a general reserve as follows:

a. Where prudential guideline provision is greater than IFRS provision, transfer the difference from the general reserve to a non-distributable regulatory reserve.

b. Where prudential guideline provision is less than IFRS provision, transfer the excess to general reserve to the extent of the amount previously transferred into the non-distributable reserve. The non-distributable reserve should be classified under Tier 1 as part of core capital.

## 17.8 Financial assets carried at cost

An unquoted equity instrument that is not carried at fair value because its fair value cannot be reliably measured, or on a derivative asset that is linked to and must be settled by delivery of such an unquoted equity instrument are measured at cost.

For such instrument, if there is objective evidence that an impairment loss has been incurred, the amount of the impairment loss is measured as the difference between the carrying amount of the financial asset and the present value of estimated future cash flows discounted at the current market rate of return for a similar financial asset. Such impairment losses are not permitted to be reversed.

## 17.9 Available-for-sale financial assets

When a decline in fair value of an available-for-sale financial asset has been recognized directly in other comprehensive income and there is objective evidence that the asset is impaired, the cumulative loss that had been recognized directly in other comprehensive income should be reclassified from equity and recognized in profit or loss even though the financial asset has not been derecognized.

It is not appropriate to allocate part of the reduction below cost to impairment and part to a fair value movement through other comprehensive income.

The amount of cumulative loss that is recycled to profit or loss is the difference between the acquisition cost (net of any principal repayment and amortization) and current fair value, less any impairment loss on that financial asset previously recognized in profit or loss.

Any portion of the cumulative net loss that is attributable to foreign currency changes on that asset that had been recognized in equity is also recognized in profit or loss.

Subsequent losses, including any portion attributable to foreign currency changes are also recognized in profit or loss until the asset is derecognized.

### 17.10 Objective Evidence of impairment

IAS 39 provides examples of factors that may, either individually or taken together, provide sufficient objective evidence that an impairment loss has been incurred in a financial asset or group of financial assets.

They include observable data that come to the attention of the holder of the asset about the following loss events:

- Significant financial difficulty of the issuer or obligor
- A breach of contract, such as a default in interest or principal payments
- The lender, for economic or legal reasons relating to the borrower's financial difficulty, granting to the borrower a concession that the lender would not otherwise consider
- It becoming probable that the borrower will enter bankruptcy or other financial reorganization
- The disappearance of an active market for that financial asset because of financial difficulties
- Observable data indicating that there is a measurable decrease in the estimated future cash flows from a group of financial assets since the initial recognition of those assets, although the decrease cannot yet be identified with the individual financial assets in the group, including adverse changes in the payment status of borrowers in the group (for example, an increased number of delayed payments or an increased number of credit card borrowers who have reached their credit limit and are paying the minimum monthly amount) or national or local economic conditions that correlate with defaults on the assets in the group (for example, an increase in the unemployment rate in the geographical area of the borrowers, a decrease in property

prices for mortgages in the relevant area, a decrease in oil prices for loan assets to oil producers, or adverse changes in industry conditions that affect the borrowers in the group)

- A downgrade of an entity's credit rating is not, of itself, evidence of impairment, although it may be evidence of impairment when considered with other available information. Other factors that an entity considers in determining whether it has objective evidence that an impairment loss has been incurred include information about:

    i. The debtors' or issuers' liquidity
    ii. Solvency, business and financial risk exposures
    iii. Levels of and trends in delinquencies for similar financial assets
    iv. National and local economic trends and conditions
    v. The fair value of collateral and guarantees.

These and other factors may, either individually or taken together, provide sufficient objective evidence that an impairment loss has been incurred in a financial asset or group of financial assets.

A decline in the fair value of a financial asset below its cost or amortized cost is not necessarily evidence of impairment (for example, a decline in the fair value of an investment in a debt instrument that results from an increase in the risk-free interest rate). Also, the disappearance of an active market because an entity's financial instruments are no longer publicly traded is not evidence of impairment.

## 17.11 Evidence of impairment for equity instruments

The standard provides additional guidance about impairment indicators that are specific to investments in equity instruments. They apply in addition to the impairment indicators described above, which focus on the assessment of impairment in debt instruments.

The additional impairment indicators that may indicate that the equity investment's cost may not be recovered are:

- Significant adverse changes in the technological, market,

economic or legal environment in which the issuer operates. Such changes include but are not limited to:

i. Structural changes in the industry or industries in which the issuer operates, such as changes in production technology or the number of competitors.
ii. Changes in the level of demand for the goods or services sold by the issuer resulting from factors such as changing consumer tastes or product obsolescence.
iii.Changes in the political or legal environment affecting the issuer's business, such as enactment of new environment protection, tax or trade laws.
iv. Changes in the issuer's financial condition evidenced by changes in factors such as its liquidity, credit rating, profitability, cash flows, debt/equity ratio and level of dividend payments.

• A significant or prolonged decline in the fair value of an investment in an equity instrument below its cost.

### 17.12 Tax Implications

The classifications of financial instruments suggest that some of the instruments are held for trading rather than for investments and capital appreciation purpose.

**a. Revenue**
• Financial Assets (FVTPL): Profits or losses recognized on the profit or loss statements could be deemed to be a revenue transaction therefore liable to income tax.
• Financial Assets (HTM): The income earned in form of interests or dividends are recognized in the profit or loss statement. Interest is liable to income tax while dividend is treated as franked investment income.
• Loan and Receivables: The interest would be liable to income tax
• Available-for-sale assets: The gains and losses being recognized on the other comprehensive income would qualify as capital gain and

therefore exempted from income tax and capital gains tax
- Financial liabilities: Interest payments would qualify for allowable deductions for income tax purpose but subject to WHT deductions. Dividend payment is appropriation of profit to be reported in statement of changes in equity, WHT will be deducted at source and the entity may be required to pay Tax on dividend.

## b. Impairment
- Impairment test resulting to impairment loss carried on individual assets are specific and therefore allowed for income tax purposes.
- Impairment test on collective assets with similar credit risk suggest general provisions and not normally allowed for tax purposes. This is because specific evidence to satisfy the Revenue may not exist.
- Impairment provision based on age analysis of debts is not allowed under the IFRS and is regarded as general provision; however, the FIRS usually regard such provisions as specific provisions for tax purposes.
- The CBN classification of non-performing loans for both specialized and non-specialized loans are general provision under the IFRS. The FIRS usually treat such provision as specific provision for income tax purposes.

## c. Tax waiver on bonds and short term securities
The new CITA and VAT gazettes exempt the income or gains realized from trading on corporate and government bonds, treasury bills and other short term securities for the period of ten years effective January 2nd, 2012.

### References
IFRS RED Book 2011 PART A: 'the conceptual framework and requirements' and PART B: 'the accompanying documents'
    IAS 32 Financial Instruments: Presentation
    IAS 39 Financial Instruments: Recognition and Measurement
    IFRS 7 Financial Instruments: Disclosure
CBN Prudential Guideline July 2010
Companies Income Tax Act Cap C21 2004 LFN
Midaspage, Nigeria (2010) Tax Consequences of Adopting IFRS in Nigeria
Companies Income Tax Exemption Order January 2nd 2012
Value Added Tax (modification) Order January 2nd 2012

# IFRS 4: Insurance Contracts

## 18.1 Introduction

IFRS 4 is the first international accounting standard to deal with insurance contracts. This is to make some improvements to accounting for insurance contracts and to ensure that insurance companies disclose certain information about insurance contracts.

The scope of the standard covers insurance contracts (including reinsurance contracts) that an entity issues and to reinsurance contracts that it holds. It also covers financial instruments issued with a discretionary participation feature. IFRS 4 does not apply to:

- Financial assets and liabilities within the scope of IAS 39
- Other assets and liabilities of an insurance company
- Product warranties issued by manufacturer, dealer or retailer
- Employers' assets and liabilities under employee benefit plans
- Contractual rights or obligations such as residual value guarantee embedded in a finance lease
- Financial guarantee not explicitly regarded as insurance contracts
- Contingent consideration payable or receivable in a business combination
- Direct insurance contracts in which the insurance company is the policy holder.

## 18.2 Bundled Insurance Contracts

Where an insurance company issues a contract that has both insurance and deposit components, the insurer will be required to unbundle the contract into separate components if the following conditions are met.

- The insurer can measure the deposit component separately without the insurance component and its accounting policies do not require it to recognize obligations and rights associated with the deposit.
- The insurer may unbundle the component if its accounting policies require it to recognize obligations and rights associated with the deposit which can be measured separately.
- The insurer should not unbundle a contract if the deposit component cannot be measured separately.
- To unbundle a contract, an insurer shall apply IFRS 4 to the insurance component and IFRS 9 to the deposit component.
- IFRS 9 requires insurer to separate some embedded derivatives from their host contract, measure them at fair value and reflect them in profit or loss except where the embedded derivative is an insurance contract.

### 18.3 Recognition and measurement

**a. Temporary Exemptions:** IFRS 4 exempts an insurer temporarily from some requirements of other IFRSs especially IAS 8 Accounting Policies, Changes in Accounting Estimates and Errors, including the consideration of IASB framework in selecting accounting policies for insurance contracts. It exempts an insurer from the application of accounting policies for:

- Insurance contracts that it issues including related acquisition costs and related intangible assets, and
- Reinsurance contracts that it holds.

**b. Prohibition:** IFRS 4 does not permit an insurer to
Recognize any provision for possible claims under contracts that are not in existence at the end of the reporting period e.g. provision for unexpired risk etc.

- Remove insurance liabilities from its statement of financial position until they are discharged or cancelled or expired.
- Offset insurance liability against reinsurance assets.
- Offset income or expense from reinsurance contracts against the expense or income from the related insurance contracts.

**c. Liability Adequacy Test:** An insurer should assess at each reporting date whether adequate insurance liability has been recognized in the financial statement based on the current estimates of future cash flows from the insurance contracts.

If the assessment shows that the carrying amount of its insurance liabilities (less related deferred acquisition costs and related intangible assets) is inadequate in the light of the estimated future cash flows, the entire deficiency shall be recognized in the profit or loss statement.

**d. Impairment Test:** An insurer shall consider whether its reinsurance assets are impaired at each reporting date and recognize any impairment loss in the profit or loss statement. A reinsurance asset is impaired if:

- there is objective evidence, as a result of an event that occurred after initial recognition of the reinsurance asset, that the cedant may not receive all amounts due to it under the terms of the contract.
- the event has a reliably measurable impact on the amounts that the cedant will receive from the reinsurer.

## 18.4 Tax implications

IFRS 4 identifies long-term insurance contracts, short-term insurance contracts and investment contracts which are covered under other accounting standards. The specific products under long-term insurance contracts are mostly life assurance policies while other risk policies are regarded as short-term insurance contracts.

Section 16 of the Companies Income Tax Act Cap C21 2004 LFN classifies insurance business as life and general insurance businesses. The following are the tax implications on insurance contracts.

**Composite Insurance Business:** Under the Nigerian Tax Law, any insurer carrying out life and general insurance business is deemed to be engaged in two separate businesses. Though only one financial statement is usually prepared for the company, two tax returns are required to be filed with the Revenue. Further, losses incurred in any class of business can only be offset against profit of the same class of business or insurance contract. Losses can be carried forward and relieved against future profits of the same business for up to four years of assessment.

**Premium Received by insurer:** Under the life assurance business, premium received from policyholders are not regarded as taxable income. However premium is a taxable income under general insurance business. This practice will be same under IFRS reporting framework. Allowance is however made for premium ceded to Reinsurance Company before assessing premium to tax under general business.

**Claims Paid to Policyholders:** Claims paid are not allowable deductions under life assurance business but are allowed under general business. This would remain the same under IFRS reporting framework. Adjustment is required for claims received from Reinsurance Company.

**Investment income:** IFRS 4 identifies investment contracts which are accounted for under IFRS 9 financial instruments. Gains or losses from the fair value of such investments are reported in the profit or loss statement. Investment income will also include: rental income, interest, commission, dividend liable to income tax etc. Dividends are treated as franked investment income and are exempted from tax.

**Actuarial Valuations:** IFRS 4 also permits actuarial valuations. The revaluation surplus on life insurance contract realized or credited to the income statement are taxable income under the Companies Income Tax Act. Actuarial gains and losses on defined benefit plans are recognized in other comprehensive income.

**Transfer to reserves and provisions:** The Companies Income Tax Act permits the following transfer to reserves and provisions:

**a. Life Business:** An annual transfer to the life fund or general reserve not exceeding net liabilities on policies in force at the time of actuarial valuation. Also, an annual provision transfer to special reserve being the higher of 1%       of gross premium and 10% of net profit. These are treated as allowable deductions for tax purpose.

**b. General Business:** A deduction of provision for unexpired risk on policies restricted to 25% of gross premium for cargo marine contracts and 45% of gross premium on other insurance contracts.

The above provisions or transfer to reserves are directives of the Insurance Act 2003 and National Insurance Commission policy guidelines. IFRS 4 does not permit recognition of provision for future claims not existing at the reporting date or any equalization provision. It however recommends insurer to carry out liability adequacy test.

**c. Liability Adequacy Test:** At each reporting date, insurers are to assess the adequacy of their insurance liabilities in the financial statement, using current estimates of future cash flows from insurance contracts and recognize any deficiency in the profit or loss statement. The tax law only permits the deductions of specific provisions to the extent that they are reliably estimated.

**Impairment of reinsurance asset:** A cedant is required to carry out impairment test of its assets ceded under reinsurance contract and recognize any impairment loss in the profit or loss statement. Impairment loss reported in the income statement is not tax deductible for income tax purpose.

**Restrictions of allowable expenses:** There is a restriction of 25% of gross premium as the allowable expenses deductible in any year of assessment for an insurer carrying out general insurance business under the Companies Income Tax Act Cap C21 2004 LFN.

**Payment of Information Levy:** The National Information Development Agency Act 2007 requires insurance companies to pay 1% of their profit before tax as IT levy. The IT levy is tax deductible when paid.

Minimum Tax: Effective 2007, insurance companies are required to pay minimum tax. The applicable effective rates are 6% of total/gross income for life assurance business and 4.5% of total/gross income for general or non-life business.

### References

IFRS RED Book 2012 PART A: 'the conceptual framework and requirements' and PART B: 'the accompanying documents'
  IFRS 4 Insurance Contracts
Companies Income Tax Act Cap C21 2004 LFN
Midaspage, Nigeria (2010) Tax Consequences of Adopting IFRS in Nigeria

# IFRS 6: Exploration for Evaluation of Mineral Resources Operations (IFRS)

## 19.1 Introduction

IFRS 6 deals with the recognition of assets used in the exploration and evaluation of mineral resources and the assessment of the assets for impairment but however excludes:

- Any other aspects of accounting by entities engaged in the exploration for and evaluation of mineral resources.
- Any expenditure incurred before the entity has obtained the legal rights to explore specific areas.
- Any expenditure incurred after the technical feasibility and commercial viability of extracting mineral resources are demonstrable.

An entity in developing its accounting policies for recognizing exploration and evaluation assets is permitted not to adjust the amount recognized in its financial statements to reflect non-adjusting events after the reporting period.

## 19.2 Recognition and Measurement

Exploration and evaluation assets should be measured at cost.

**Initial Cost:** The following expenditures should be recognized as part of initial cost of exploration and evaluation assets:

- Acquisition of right to explore
- Topographical, geological, geochemical and geophysical studies
- Exploratory drilling
- Trenching
- Sampling

- Evaluating the technical feasibility and commercial viability of extracting a mineral resource.
- Any obligations for removal and restoration that are incurred during a particular period as a consequence of having undertaken exploration and evaluation of mineral resources should be recognized in accordance with IAS 37.
- Any expenditure relating to the development of mineral resources after the technical feasibility and commercial viability has been established including administrative or general overheads will not form part of the cost of the asset.

**Scenario 19.1: Recognition of Initial cost.**
Excel Hydrocarbon Ltd is an oil producing company which has just acquired oil prospecting licence in Nigeria to engage in exploration and development activities. The company paid N5million to obtain the license and incurred N17million on topographical, geological and geophysical studies to evaluate the commercial viability of the oil prospecting area. The survey report revealed that up to five oil wells could be developed in the area; however, N450million has been incurred to develop four wells in the first financial year. Evaluate financial statement and tax effects.

Excel Hydrocarbon Ltd would recognize N472million as the initial cost of exploration and evaluation asset which covers the cost incurred on acquisition right to explore, exploratory drilling, and topographical, geological and geophysical studies.

The qualifying capital expenditure for capital allowance purpose would be N455million referred to as tangible drilling cost which covers the acquisition of right to explore and exploratory drilling. Intangible drilling amounting to N6.8million for the drilling of the first two appraisal wells will be tax deductible while N10.2million of the intangible drilling costs will not be tax deductible for petroleum profit tax purpose.

**Subsequent cost:** An entity may choose to apply cost model or revaluation model to measure its exploration and evaluation assets in accordance with IAS 16 and IAS 38.

### 19.3 Impairment of Assets

Exploration and evaluation of assets shall be assessed for impairment annually in accordance with IAS 36 and any impairment loss should be recognized as an expense in the profit or loss statement.

An entity should measure and disclose any impairment loss when facts and circumstances suggest that the carrying amount exceeds the recoverable amount. For the purpose of exploration and evaluation assets, the following are facts and circumstances that may indicate whether an asset or a cash generating unit is impaired:

- The entity's right to explore in a specific area has expired or will expire in the near future and there are no intentions of renewals
- There is no plan or budget to incur substantive expenditure for further exploration in a specific area.
- The entity has decided to discontinue exploration activities due to non-discovery of commercially viable quantities of mineral resources in a specific area.
- There is objective evidence or sufficient data that the carrying amount of the assets is unlikely to be recovered in full from successful development or sale of a specific area.
- The entity has made plans to sell the exploration and evaluation asset at an unfavourable price.

### 19.4 Tax Implications

Companies engaged in exploration and production of crude oil are assessed to tax under the Petroleum Profit Tax Act Cap P13 2004 LFN. IFRS 6 recognition of expenditure as cost of exploration and evaluation asset differs from qualifying capital expenditures for capital allowance purpose. The Act recognizes the following qualifying capital expenditures:

- Plant: Expenditure on Plants, Machinery and fixtures
- Pipeline and storage: Capital expenditure incurred on pipeline and storage tanks
- Building: Capital expenditure on the construction of buildings, structures or works of a permanent nature
- Drilling: Capital expenditure in respect of acquisition of rights in or over petroleum deposits, searching for, or discovering and testing deposits and construction of any works or structure which are likely to be of little use when petroleum operation ceases.

For petroleum profit tax purpose, drilling cost is classified as tangible drilling cost and intangible drilling cost.

- Tangible drilling costs are qualifying capital expenditure on which capital allowance can be claimed. It covers acquisition of right to explore, exploratory drilling, trenching sampling or testing for petroleum deposit.

- Intangible drilling costs for the first two appraisal wells in a particular oil field are tax deductible. This covers, topographical, geological, geophysical studies, evaluation of technical feasibility and commercial viability or survey preparatory to drilling.

The above distinction of tangible and intangible drilling cost will impact on deferred tax. Since IFRS 6 requires capitalization of the intangible drilling cost, the Petroleum Profit Tax Act treats substantial part of the intangible drilling cost as tax deductible for income tax purpose. Also, not all the drilling cost would qualify for capital allowance purpose.

Any impairment loss charged to profit or loss statement would not be tax deductible and will also impact on the deferred tax account of the reporting entity.

## References

IFRS RED Book 2012 PART A: 'the conceptual framework and requirements' and PART B: 'the accompanying documents'
    IFRS 6 Exploration for and Evaluation of Mineral Resources
Petroleum Profit Tax Act Cap P13 2004 LFN

# IAS 12: Income Taxes

## 20.1 Introduction

IAS 12 Income Taxes is the accounting standard that deals with both current and deferred taxes.

## 20.2 Current Tax

- Current tax is the amount of income tax payable or recoverable in respect of the taxable profit or loss for a period. At the end of a reporting period, an estimated amount usually by applying the corporation tax rate in force, to accrue for the amount of tax payable based on the year's profits. The tax charge is accounted as follows:

  Dr. Profit or Loss Statement
  Cr. Tax Payable

- When the tax is actually paid some months later, it is unlikely to be the same amount as that accrued. An over-provision or under-provision is therefore left on the tax payable account.

- An over-provision arises where the actual tax paid is less than the estimated tax charged. This reduces the following year's tax charge in the profit or loss statement.

- An under-provision arises where the actual tax paid is more than the estimated tax charged. This increases the following year's tax charge in the profit or loss statement.

## 20.3 Deferred Tax

Deferred tax is the tax consequences of future recovery/settlement of the carrying amount of assets/liabilities that are recognized in an entity's statement of financial position.

Deferred tax is not a current liability or an asset to or from the tax authorities; rather, it is an accounting adjustment. Deferred tax arises because the profit before tax for accounting purposes is not the same amount as taxable profits for taxation purposes. Deferred tax:

- Recognizes the future tax effect of income or an expense in the period in which the income or expense is recognized (an application of accruals).
- Recognizes future tax expenses immediately, so ensuring that profits are not overstated (an application of prudence).
- Ensures that accounting profits are not distorted by the effects of tax. If deferred tax were ignored then a company's tax charge may bear very little resemblance to the reported profits.

There are two reasons why taxable profits and accounting profits are not the same. They are:

**a. Permanent differences:** Amounts which represent income or expenses for accounting purposes, but are not taxable/allowed for tax purposes. Example includes non-deductible donations, exempt income etc.

**b. Timing differences:** Amounts which represent income or an expense for accounting purposes and for tax purposes but in different periods. Examples include:

- Depreciation for accounting purposes vs. capital allowances for tax purposes: both write off the cost of asset but at different rates.
- Certain provisions which are tax deductible only when the related expense is paid.
- Income accounted for when receivable but not taxed until received.

## 20.4 Computation of Deferred Tax

IAS 12 (revised) prohibits the use of the deferral or the income statement liability method to determine deferred tax and prefers the balance sheet liability approach to calculate temporary differences.

The income statement liability method focuses on the timing differences, which is the difference between items considered in arriving at taxable profit and accounting profit that originate in one period and reverses in one or more subsequent periods.

The balance sheet liability approach focuses on temporary differences which involves comparing the 'carrying value' of assets or liabilities with their 'tax base' in the statement of financial position.

a. **Temporary differences:** are differences between the carrying value of an asset or liability in the statement of financial position and its tax base. Temporary differences may be either:

- *Taxable temporary differences:* are temporary differences that will result in taxable amounts in determining taxable profit (tax loss) in future periods when the carrying value of the asset or liability is recovered or settled; or
- *Deductible temporary differences:* are temporary differences that will result in amounts that are deductible in determining taxable profit (tax loss) in future periods when the carrying amount of the asset or liability is recovered or settled.

b. **Tax base:** is the amount attributed to that asset or liability for tax purposes. For example, the tax base of a non-current asset is its tax written down value (cost less cumulative capital allowances).

c. **Carrying value:** is the amount at which an asset is recognized after deducting any accumulated depreciation and accumulated impairment losses.
- Deferred tax adjusts for the effects of temporary differences, but

not permanent differences. In order to account for deferred tax, the following approach should be taken:

- Calculate the temporary difference.
- Apply the tax rate to the temporary difference in order to calculate the deferred tax liability (or asset).
- Recognize the deferred tax liability (or asset) in the financial statements.

|  | Asset | Liability |
|---|---|---|
| Carrying amount > Tax base | DT Liability | DT Asset |
| Carrying amount < Tax base | DT Asset | DT Liability |

Figure 20.1: Deferred Tax Matrix

## 20.5 Recognition of Deferred Tax

### a. Taxable temporary difference

- Deferred tax liabilities: are the amounts of income taxes payable in future periods in respect of taxable temporary differences.
- A deferred tax liability should be recognized for all taxable temporary differences except for initial recognition of goodwill and initial recognition of asset and liability in a non-business combination transaction which did not affect accounting or taxable profit.
- Deferred tax liability should be recognized for all taxable temporary difference associated with investments in subsidiaries, branches and associates and interest in joint ventures provided the parent, investor or venture can control the timing of the reversal of the temporary difference and it is probable that the temporary difference will not reverse in the foreseeable future.

### b. Deductible temporary difference

- Deferred tax assets are the amounts of income taxes recoverable in future periods in respect of deductible temporary difference, the carry forward of unused tax losses and the carry forward of unused tax credits.

- A deferred tax asset should be recognized for all deductible temporary difference to the extent that it is probable that taxable profit will be available against which the deductible temporary difference can be utilized, unless the deferred tax asset arises from the initial recognition of an asset or liability in a non-business combination transaction which did not affect accounting or taxable profit/loss.

- Deferred tax asset should be recognized for all deductible temporary difference arising from investments in subsidiaries, branches and associates, and interest in joint ventures, provided the temporary difference will reverse in the foreseeable future and the taxable profit will be available for which the temporary difference can be utilized.

- Unused tax losses and unused tax credits: A deferred tax asset shall be recognized for the carry forward of unused tax losses and unused tax credits to the extent that it is probable that future taxable profit will be available for which the unused tax loss and credit can be utilized.

## 20.6 Measurement of Deferred Tax

Deferred tax assets and liabilities should reflect the tax consequences that would follow the manner to recover or settle the carrying amount of assets and liabilities. Deferred tax is measured using the tax rates that are expected to apply when assets are realized or liabilities are settled.

The carrying value of an asset can be recovered either through sale or use. The tax rate and tax base used to measure deferred tax should be consistent with the manner of the recovery or settlement of the asset or liability.

Deferred tax is applied on non-depreciable assets measured under the revaluation model and investment properties measured under the fair model as follows:

- Non-depreciable assets revalued are to be recovered only through sale. The tax rate and the tax base to be used to measure deferred tax should be the applicable tax rate assuming the asset will be sold at the end of the reporting period.

- Investment properties carried at fair value are assumed to be recovered through sale. Deferred tax is recognized using the rate assuming that investment property will be recovered through sale at the end of the reporting period.

### Scenario 20.1: Deferred Tax

Evaluate the deferred tax effects stating how the balances will be presented/disclosed in the Financial Statement assuming 30% tax rate for recovery/settlement of assets/liabilities through use and 10% through sale on the following account balances.

1. An item of PPE which comprises land and building has a carrying amount of N42million. The building has a tax base of N18million. The cost of the land is N15million with a current fair value of N28million. Cost model is applied for this class of PPE.
2. A company has a machine with a carrying value of N17.2million and with a tax written down value of N16 million
3. A company has provided for environmental cleaning cost of N8million and this has been disallowed for tax purpose.
4. The tax computation results to carry forward loss of N5million.
5. An investment property with an initial cost of N32.7million is carried at N54million at year end.
6. The book value of financial asset classified as 'available for sale' is N9million as at 1st January 2010 and by year end the market value of the asset is N10.5million.
7. During the year impairment loss of N3million was charged to income statement in respect of an item of PPE acquired for

N15million. The accumulated depreciation at year end was N4million while total capital claimed so far on the asset was N5million.

8. The carrying amount of inventory is N23.8million. Inventories are direct cost deductible for tax purpose.

9. A special purpose plant has a tax base of N47.2 million. In the current year a revaluation surplus of N30million in excess of the tax base was credited to other comprehensive income. 25% of the temporary differences can be attributed to carrying amount of asset. No adjustment has been made for tax purpose.

10. The carrying amount of a defined benefit plan to the annual obligation at the reporting date is N98million. The carrying amount was N89million in the previous year.

Deferred Tax is computed as the tax effect on temporary difference. Temporary difference (TD) is the difference between the carry value (CV) and the tax base (TB) of an asset or a liability.

| S/N | Assets/Liabilities | CV- TB = TD<br>N'000 | Tax Effect on TD<br>@ 30% or 10% |
|-----|--------------------|----------------------|-----------------------------------|
| 1a | Building (42-15) | 27,000-18,000= 9,000 | 2,700 DT Liability |
| 1b | Land@ Cost | 15,000-15,000=0 | Nil |
| 1c | Land @ Fair Value | 28,000-15,000=13,000 | 1,300 DT Liability |
| 2 | PPE | 17,200-16,000=1,200 | 360 DT Liability |
| 3 | Environment Cleaning Cost | (8,000)- 0= (8,000) | 2,400 DT Asset |
| 4 | Tax Loss | 0-(5,000)= (5,000) | 1,500 DT Asset |
| 5 | Investment Property | 54,000-32,700=21,300 | 2,130 DT Liability |
| 6 | Financial Asset | 10,500-9,000 = 1,500 | 450 DT Liability |
| 7 | PPE (15-3-4) | 8,000-10,000=(2,000) | 600 DT Asset |
| 8 | Inventory | 23,800-23,800=0 | Nil |
| 9 | Plant (30 + 47.2) | 77,200-47,200=30,000<br>P/L (25%*9000)<br>OCI (75%*9000) | <br>2,250 DT Liability<br>6,750 DT Liability |
| 10 | Employee benefit | 98,000-89,000=9,000 | 2,700 DT Asset |

### Deferred Tax Analysis

| | |
|---|---|
| Deferred Tax Liability | 7,440,000 |
| Deferred Tax Asset | (4,500,000) |
| Charge to Profit or Loss for the year | 2,940,000 |

### Deferred Tax Charge to OCI

| | |
|---|---|
| Financial Asset | 450,000 |
| Revalued Plant | 6,750,000 |
| | 7,200,000 |

### Notes on Deferred Tax

The non-depreciable asset (Land) is currently carried at cost, however as at the reporting date deferred tax liability amounts to N1, 300,000.00, which represents the fair value of the land if the carry value of the land were to be recovered at that date.

The deferred tax on financial assets available for sale reflects the gains and loss arising from fair value measurement; this may be ignored as the gains arising from derecognition or disposal of the financial assets will be exempted from tax.

### References

IFRS RED Book 2012 PART A: 'the conceptual framework and requirements' and PART B: 'the accompanying documents'
    IAS 12 Income Taxes
Midaspage, Nigeria (2010) Tax Consequences of Adopting IFRS in Nigeria

## Chapter 2
## Appendix 1: Exception and exemption from retrospective application

| Mandatory exceptions from full retrospective application | Scope – exception applies to |
|---|---|
| Estimates | All Estimates |
| Derecognition of financial assets and liabilities | All financial assets and liabilities de-recognized before 1 January 2004 |
| Hedge accounting | All hedging relationships in existence from accounting period beginning prior to adoption of IAS39 |
| Non-controlling interests | All equity in a subsidiary not attributable, directly or indirectly, to a parent |
| **Optional exemptions from full retrospective application** | **Scope – where exemption taken, it applies to** |
| Business combinations | All business combinations, or if choose to not to apply for one combination then exemption does not apply to any combination that took place after that one. |
| Share- based payment transactions | Equity instruments granted prior to 7 November 2002 or equity instruments granted after 7 November 2002 that had not vested by later of the date of transition and1 January 2005 |
| Insurance contracts | All insurance contracts |
| Fair value or revaluation as deemed cost | Any tangible fixed asset, investment property and to a limited number of intangible assets |
| Leases | All arrangements that contain a lease |
| Employee benefits | All employee benefit plans |
| Cumulative translation differences | All cumulative translation differences existing at the date of transition to IFRS. |
| Investments in subsidiaries, joint controlled entities | Any investments in subsidiaries joint entities controlled entities and associates. |
| Assets and liabilities of subsidiaries, associates and joint ventures | All assets and liabilities of individual subsidiaries, associates and joint ventures |
| Compound financial instruments | All compound financial instruments where the liability component has been settled by the date of transition to IFRS. |
| Designation of previously recognized financial instruments | Any financial instrument. |
| Fair value measurement of financial assets or financial liabilities at initial recognition | All relevant financial assets or financial liabilities |
| Decommissioning liabilities included in the cost of property, plant and equipment. | All decommissioning liabilities |
| Financial assets or intangible assets accounted for in intangible assets accounted for with IFRIC 12, 'Service concession arrangements'. | All relevant financial assets or assets accounted for in accordance with IFRIC 12 |
| Borrowing costs | All borrowing costs |

## Chapter 3
## Appendix 1: Statement of Financial Position

| Assets | 2010 N'000 | 2009 N'000 |
|---|---|---|
| **Non-Current Assets** | | |
| Property, plant and equipment | 350 | 360 |
| Goodwill | 80 | 91 |
| Other intangible assets | 227 | 227 |
| Investments in associates | 100 | 110 |
| Investments in equity instruments | 142 | 156 |
| | 901 | 945 |
| **Current Assets** | | |
| Inventories | 135 | 132 |
| Trade receivables | 91 | 110 |
| Other current assets | 22 | 12 |
| Cash and cash equivalents | 312 | 322 |
| | 564 | 578 |
| **Total Assets** | **1,466** | **1,524** |
| | | |
| **Equity and Liabilities** | | |
| ***Equity attributable to owners of the parent*** | | |
| Share capital | 650 | 600 |
| Retained earnings | 243 | 161 |
| Other components of equity | 20 | 21 |
| | 903 | 782 |
| Non-controlling interests | 70 | 48 |
| Total equity | 973 | 831 |
| | | |
| **Non-current liabilities** | | |
| Long-term borrowings | 120 | 160 |
| Deferred tax | 28 | 26 |
| Long-term provisions | 28 | 52 |
| Total non-current liabilities | 177 | 238 |
| | | |
| **Current liabilities** | | |
| Trade and other payables | 155 | 187 |
| Short-term borrowings | 150 | 200 |
| Current portion of long-term borrowings | 10 | 20 |
| Current tax payable | 35 | 42 |
| Short-term provisions | 5 | 5 |
| Total current liabilities | 315 | 454 |
| **Total liabilities** | **492** | **692** |
| | | |
| **Total equity and liabilities** | **1,466** | **1,524** |

## Appendix 2: Statement of Profit or Loss and Other Comprehensive Income

|  | 2010 N'000 | 2009 N'000 |
|---|---|---|
| Revenue | 390 | 355 |
| Cost of sales | (245) | (230) |
| Gross profit | 145 | 125 |
| Other Income | 20 | 11 |
| Distribution cost | (9) | (8) |
| Administrative expenses | (20) | (21) |
| Other expenses | (2) | (1) |
| Finance costs | (8) | (7) |
| Share of profit of associates | 35 | 29 |
| **Profit before tax** | 161 | 128 |
| Income tax expense | (40) | (32) |
| **Profit for the year from continuing operations** | 121 | 96 |
| Loss for the year from discontinued operations | - | (31) |
| **Profit for the year** | 121 | 65 |
| **Other comprehensive income:** | | |
| Exchange difference on translating foreign operations | 5 | 10 |
| Investments in equity instruments | (23) | 26 |
| Cash flow hedges | (1) | (4) |
| Gains on property revaluation | 1 | 3 |
| Actuarial gains (losses) on defined benefit pension plan | (1) | 1 |
| Share of other comprehensive income of associates | 1 | (1) |
| Income tax relating to components of OCI | 4 | (7) |
| **Other comprehensive income for the year net of tax** | (14) | 28 |
| **Total comprehensive income for the year** | 107 | 93 |
| | | |
| Profit attributable to: | | |
| Owners of the parent | 97 | 52 |
| Non-controlling interests | 24 | 13 |
| | 121 | 65 |
| | | |
| Total comprehensive income attributable to: | | |
| Owners of the parent | 85 | 74 |
| Non-controlling interests | 22 | 19 |
| | 107 | 93 |
| Earnings per share | | |
| Basic and diluted | 0.46 | 0.30 |

*The above is the format for Statement of Comprehensive Income in a single statement and the classification of expenses within profit by function.*

**Appendix 3: Statement of Profit or Loss and Other Comprehensive Income in two statements and classification of expenses within profit by nature**

|  | 2010 N'000 | 2009 N'000 |
|---|---|---|
| Revenue | 390 | 355 |
| Other income | 20 | 1 |
| Changes in inventories of finished goods and work in progress | (115) | (107) |
| Work performed by the entity and capitalized | 16 | 15 |
| Raw material and consumables used | (96) | (92) |
| Employee benefits expense | (45) | (43) |
| Depreciation and amortization expense | (19) | (17) |
| Impairment of property, plant and equipment | (4) | - |
| Other expenses | (6) | (5) |
| Finance costs | (15) | (18) |
| Share of profit of associates | 35 | 29 |
| **Profit before tax** | 161 | 128 |
| Income tax expense | (40) | (32) |
| **Profit for the year from continuing operations** | 121 | 96 |
| Loss for the year from discontinued operations | - | (31) |
| **Profit for the year** | 121 | 65 |

**Appendix 4: Statement of Other Comprehensive Income for the year**

|  |  |  |
|---|---|---|
| Profit for the year | 121 | 65 |
| Exchange difference on translating foreign operations | 5 | 10 |
| Investments in equity instruments | (23) | 26 |
| Cash flow hedges | (1) | (4) |
| Gains on property revaluation | 1 | 3 |
| Actuarial gains (losses) on defined benefit pension plan | (1) | 1 |
| Share of other comprehensive income of associates | 1 | (1) |
| Income tax relating to components of OCI | 4 | (7) |
| **Other comprehensive income for the year net of tax** | **(14)** | **2** |
| **Total comprehensive income for the year** | **107** | **93** |

## Appendix 5: Statement of Other comprehensive income - Disclosure of Tax effects

| | 2010 N'000 | | | 2009 N'000 | | |
|---|---|---|---|---|---|---|
| | Gross | Tax | Net | Gross | Tax | Net |
| Exchange difference on translating foreign operations | 5 | 1 | 4 | 10 | (2) | 8 |
| Investments in equity instruments | (24) | 6 | (18) | 26 | (5) | 21 |
| Cash flow hedges | (1.5) | 0.5 | (1) | (4) | 1 | (3) |
| Gains on property revaluation | 1.5 | (0.5) | 1 | 3 | (1) | 2 |
| Actuarial gains (losses) on defined benefit pension plan | (1.5) | 0.5 | (1) | 2 | (1) | 1 |
| Share of other comprehensive income of associates | 2 | (1) | 1 | (4) | 3 | (1) |
| Other comprehensive income for the year net of tax | (18.5) | 4.5 | (14) | 33 | (5) | 28 |

## Appendix 6: Statement of Change in Equity

| | Share Capital | Retained Earnings | Transaction of foreign operations | Investments in equity instruments | Cash flow hedges | Revaluation surplus | Total Non | Total Controlling Interest | Equity |
|---|---|---|---|---|---|---|---|---|---|
| | N | N | N | N | N | N | N | N | N |
| Balance at 1 January 2009 | 600,000 | 118,100 | (4,000) | 1,600 | 2,000 | | 717,700 | 29,800 | 717,500 |
| Changes in accounting policy | 400 | | | | | | 400 | 100 | 500 |
| **Restated Balance** | 600,000 | 118,500 | (4,000) | 1,600 | 2,000 | | 717,700 | 29,900 | 748,000 |
| **Changes in equity for 2009** | | | | | | | | | |
| Dividend | | (10,000) | | | | | (10,000) | | |
| Total comprehensive income for the year | | 53,200 | 6,400 | 16,000 | (2,400) | 1,600 | 74,800 | 18,700 | 93,500 |
| **Balance at 31 December 2009** | 600,000 | 161,700 | 2,400 | 17,600 | (400) | 1,600 | 782,900 | 48,600 | 831,500 |
| **Changes in equity for 2010** | | | | | | | | | |
| Issue of share capital | 50,000 | | | | | | 50,000 | | 50,000 |
| Dividends | | (15,000) | | | | | (15,000) | | (15,000) |
| Total comprehensive income for the year | | 96,600 | 3,200 | (14,400) | (400) | 800 | 85,800 | 21,450 | 107,250 |
| Transfer to Retained Earnings | | 200 | | | | | | | |
| **Balance at 31 December 2010** | 650,000 | 243,500 | 5,600 | 3,200 | (800) | 2,200 | 903,700 | 70,050 | 973,750 |

# Index

171